IMAGES OF ENGLAND

CROYDON CINEMAS

THE
CREAMERY
TEA ROOMS
& RESTAURANT.

TEA ROOMS
AND
RESTAURANT

Afternoon Teas

STATION PICTURE HALL.

The Creamery

CONTINUOUS
PERFORMANCE
EVENINGS.
6.30 till 11.
AFTERNOONS
3 till 5.

AFTERNOON
PERFORMANCE
MONDAYS
TH

IMAGES OF ENGLAND

CROYDON CINEMAS

ALLEN EYLES

ASSISTED BY

KEITH SKONE

TEMPUS

Frontispiece: The Station Picture Hall (courtesy of John Gent – CTA/ Tony Moss Collection).

Front cover: ABC Croydon, October 1965.

Back cover: The Coulsdon Cinema being prepared for one of its many re-openings in the late 1920s. (John Gent Collection.)

First published 2006

Tempus Publishing Limited
The Mill, Brimscombe Port,
Stroud, Gloucestershire, GL5 2QG
www.tempus-publishing.com

British Library Cataloguing in Publication Data.
A catalogue record for this book is available from the British Library.

ISBN 0 7524 3816 6

Typesetting and origination by Tempus Publishing Limited.
Printed in Great Britain.

Contents

Acknowledgements

In revising this history of the Borough of Croydon's cinemas, I have been particularly indebted to Richard Norman, who was immensely helpful in accessing images from the collection of the late Tony Moss during the transitional period of its handover to the Cinema Theatre Association (CTA). He also provided some images of his own, and liaised on my behalf with John Gent, the doyen of Croydon historians, who has kindly supplied some invaluable new images from his collection.

The Cinema Theatre Association Archive (Clive Polden and Rachel Marks) has again rallied to my support. It was rewarding to use the Local History section of the new Croydon Library for newspaper research.

I reiterate my thanks to the following who assisted with information and illustrations, support or other encouragement when this history was first published (in a different format) in 1989: Arthur Carter, Mrs Chipperfield, Cinema Theatre Association Archive (David Jones), Harry Collier (manager of the Savoy/ABC Croydon, 1952-80), John Collins (ex-manager, Davis Theatre), Gordon Coombes, *Croydon Advertiser,* Mrs Rose Dawson, Joyce Day (last manageress of the Odeon Croydon), John Fernée, Jack Gill, Richard Gray, Anna Knox, Robert Murphy, Michael Thomas, Eric Tripp (manager, Granada Thornton Heath, 1965/66), Mrs M. Turnell, and staff of the Local History Unit, Croydon Public Libraries. In addition, co-publisher and cinema and organ expert Tony Moss added many details which are directly quoted in the text.

The 1989 publication produced instructive letters from C.J. Bird, Russell F. Burstow, John House and K.A. Vaughan, and the information they provided has been incorporated into this new history. I have also drawn on some incidental titbits from Jon Burrows, both directly and from his invaluable, recently published, two-part research into London cinemas of the 1906-1914 period, 'Penny Pleasures', published in *Film History* Vol. 16: 1 and 2, 2004. And a 1989 article uncovered by Richard Norman, 'The Riddle of Coulsdon's Cinema' by Tony Newman of the Bourne Society, helped clarify that site's still muddled history. Spencer P. Hobbs kindly filled in details of the cinema at Crystal Palace from his exhaustive research into the Borough of Bromley's cinemas.

All photographs not credited to specific collections are from the collections of the author and his research associate, Keith Skone. Even though this history of Croydon cinemas is an improvement on its 1989 predecessor, there is more information and more illustrations out there somewhere. Any corrections, reminiscences and discoveries of further interesting photographs (especially interiors) will be welcomed to enhance future editions.

Readers interested in the history of cinemas should consider joining the CTA, established in 1967, which not only maintains an archive but organises visits and lectures and publishes a bi-monthly newsletter and annual magazine. Details are available from www.cinema-theatre.org.uk or Membership Secretary, Flat One, No. 128 Gloucester Terrace, London W2 6HP.

A note on money

The text refers to many prices of admission in pre-decimalisation money: pounds (£), shillings (s) and pence (d) so that 2s 6d means two shillings and sixpence. One present penny is the approximate equivalent of two and a half old pence. Five pence today are the equivalent of the old twelve pence known as a shilling. The old one shilling and sixpence is worth seven and a half new pence. A pound is still a pound but it used to be worth twenty shillings or 240 pence.

Introduction

It was on 20 February 1896 that the first paying audience went to the cinema in Britain. A presentation of short films made by the Lumière brothers in France was such a success at the Marlborough Hall in Regent Street that it was taken up by the Empire music hall in Leicester Square as an item on its variety bill from 9 March. A rival film show, Robert W. Paul's Theatrograph (later Animatograph), made an appearance at another Leicester Square music hall, the Alhambra, later the same month.

By the end of the year, music halls all over the country were screening moving pictures in these two systems. In Croydon, the first recorded showing of these 'animated photographs' was at the National Palace (later Empire) Theatre from 12 October 1986, where Paul's Theatrograph appeared. (Perhaps the Theatre Royal in Crown Hill nabbed the Lumière apparatus?)

The National Palace is known to have introduced a further system, the Velograph, in 1897. In the second half of 1896, a Croydon photographic firm, Bender & Co., acquired the rights to a system called the Grand Kinematograph, using large gauge film. Ten films made in the process were shown to the Croydon Camera Club on 13 January 1897, including one of keen local interest, *Demolition of Old Railway Station, Croydon*. The apparatus was later modified to project conventional films of 35mm gauge and renamed the Velograph. It was put to commercial use by the Velograph Syndicate Ltd and (as noted by John Barnes in *The Rise of the Cinema in Great Britain*, 1983) it appeared as a special attraction on the bill at the National Palace Theatre in August 1897, celebrating Queen Victoria's Diamond Jubilee. (E.J. Dale, a noted magician of the day, also presented a programme of Jubilee films that month at the Crystal Palace.)

For a few years, moving pictures continued as a star feature in music hall programmes, as a travelling fairground attraction, and as a one-night novelty in meeting halls and public baths. Around 1906-8, short films were regularly presented in Croydon at the Empire (the former National Palace) and Theatre Royal, as well as on an occasional basis at the Public Hall and at the YMCA's Horniman Hall in North End.

When it was clear that films were not just a passing novelty, the first proper cinemas were established, usually created in existing buildings. The earliest example of this in Croydon occurred in 1908, but the Theatre Royal and Empire Theatre continued to show films, contracting with American Bioscope and Imperial Bioscope respectively for a regular supply of material. Another source of programmes, Standard Pictures, had its releases presented at the Stanley Halls in South Norwood from time to time (this never became a full-time cinema).

Historian Jon Burrows informs me that a surviving police report from 'W' Division (Brixton, south London) notes that on 23 March 1909 the police found a bioscope exhibition operating

THE NATIONAL

PALACE THEATRE

of Varieties, Croydon.

Lessees:—THE NATIONAL PALACE OF VARIETIES, CROYDON (LTD.).

Directors:—Messrs. HERBERT CAMPBELL, DAN LENO,
HARRY RANDALL, FRED WILLIAMS, HENRY JOYNER, and
G. E. S. VENNER.

General Manager: Mr. J. SPARROW.   Resident Manager: Mr. F. A. LENNON.
Secretary: Mr. G. E. S. VENNER.

⋙ PROGRAMME ⋘

FOR

MONDAY, AUGUST 9th, 1897,

AND EVERY EVENING DURING THE WEEK.

1   OVERTURE
            (Band).

2   The SISTERS DE CASTRO AND
        MAUD STONEHAM,
    In Novel Musical Sketch, entitled—
    "HIS LORDSHIP."

3   Miss EMMA CHAMBERS,
    (The Popular Comedienne and Burlesque Actress).

4   The McCONNELL FAMILY,
        In Operatic Trios, &c.

5 Miss LILY WELFORD (Serio & Speciality Dancer)

6   Special and Most Expensive Engagement of

THE VELOGRAPH

Series of ANIMATED PHOTOGRAPHS. A Selection from the following
Views will be shown Every Evening :—

THE DIAMOND JUBILEE

(The Procession in its entirety). Her Majesty the Queen and Royal Family at
the State Garden Party, Buckingham Palace. The Royal Regatta,
Henley 1897—The Derby, 1897—The Ascot Gold Cup, 1897—The Flying
Scotchman—The Seaside—Military Drill—London Life—and others.

7   The FIGAROS
    (Continental Operatic Duettists and Dancers).

8   Lieut. WALTER COLE
    (The Great Ventriloquist, with his "Merry Folks.").

9   Mr. GEORGE BEAUCHAMP
        (The Great Comic Vocalist).

10 Professor ROBERT GILBERT'S
    TROUPE OF ACROBATIC DOGS,
        Introducing Novel and Original Tricks.

11   REZENE AND ROBINI
        (Burlesque Trapeze Artistes).

"GOD SAVE THE QUEEN."

Musical Director: Mr. LEON A. BASSETT.
Stage Manager: Mr. J. CROWLEY.

THIS PROGRAMME IS SUBJECT TO ALTERATION.

The Numbers Shown from the sides of the Stage will correspond
with those on the Programme.

Pianoforte supplied by G. and A. WEBB.

Doors open at 7.30.   Commence at 7.45.
Saturdays, Early Doors at 6.45.   Commence 7.30.   Extra Talent.

In this 1897 programme for Croydon's National Palace Theatre of Varieties (later Empire/Eros), item six on the bill is the 'Special and Most Expensive Engagement of The Velograph. Series of Animated Photographs. A Selection from the following Views will be shown Every Evening:- The Diamond Jubilee (The Procession in its entirety). Her Majesty the Queen and Royal Family at the State Garden Party, Buckingham Palace. The Royal Regatta, Henley 1897 – The Derby, 1897 – The Ascot Gold Cup 1897 – The Flying Scotchman – The Seaside – Military Drill – London Life – and others'.

at No. 9 Church Street, Croydon in a venue which also featured various automatic machines and a shooting range (presumably some kind of funfair or amusement arcade). This may be one of many such shows which lasted an indeterminate time and cannot be counted as proper cinemas.

From 1910, when licensing was introduced to ensure that premises showing inflammable film were suitable for the purpose (with a separate projection box and more than one exit in case of fire), there began to appear purpose-built cinemas that met these requirements and provided more spacious surroundings with seating on a properly raked floor. Most of these early cinemas proved too small and were put out of business by problems of staffing, rising costs and low attendance during the First World War or by new, larger rivals.

By 1916, existing cinemas were trying desperately to ward off further competition by opposing new planning and licensing applications. In April 1915, a barrister declared that there were already twenty-one cinemas in the borough with a seating capacity of 12,448, so that with three shows a day there was a seat available for every person in Croydon once a week. In Croydon, as in most towns, magistrates were rarely sympathetic to arguments for restraining competition, and the barrister (acting for the Scala and Croydon Cinematograph Theatres) was unsuccessful in preventing the North End Brotherhood introducing film shows at the North End Hall on Saturday nights. As this had 1,043 seats in all (ground floor and gallery), it posed a substantial threat to existing cinemas and its initial programmes dominated press advertising. However, films were soon abandoned in favour of musical concerts on Saturday evenings (according to the same barrister, there were already fifty-nine places with music licences, besides cinemas

Year unknown.

where music was necessary to accompany the silent films). The North End Hall occasionally showed films in later years – a new film on African life in October 1928 was advertised, as were one-day presentations of *The 39 Steps* on Boxing Day 1935 and *David Copperfield* in January 1939. In March 1936, it even expanded temporarily to showing films for three days from Thursday to Saturday, and is remembered for Friday and Saturday night screenings at other times before the Second World War.

Such was the draw of films that it had prompted another, very unlikely, licence application earlier in 1915. This was to show films at the Rifle Range at No. 49a George Street, where there would be no seats but sufficient floor space to allow thirty persons to stand! As the arrangements were deemed satisfactory in planning terms, the licence was granted on 21 January 1915 but, not surprisingly, there was no application for renewal in 1916.

One licensing problem that vexed all Croydon's film exhibitors was the refusal of permission to open on Sundays. Until 1931, when the Sunday Observance Act was enforced to close cinemas nationally on the Sabbath, local authorities could licence cinemas to give shows.

The first application for Sunday screenings in Croydon was debated by the council and thrown out by a huge majority in October 1911. Cinema owners sometimes defied the law and opened on Sundays, being prosecuted by the council and threatened with losing their licence. (One cinema was allowed to show films officially on Sundays in 1918-20 – this was the Weekend Picture Palace, aptly named since it did not function on weekdays.)

More Sunday applications were made. One in 1927 was supported by a petition with 24,000 signatures but it was rejected on a council vote by 34 to 11. In 1929, the council majority against

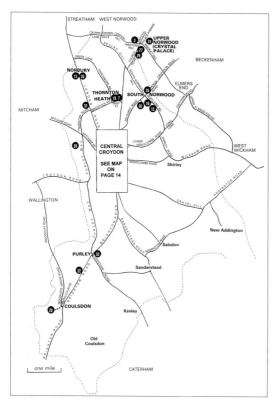

THE CINEMAS OF CROYDON
Numbered in chronological order

★3	Photodrome/Electra/Electric/Palladium
7	Electric Palace
12	Central Hall/Central/Rex
13	Palais de Luxe/Cinema/Searchlight
16	New Electric/Mascot/La Rosa/ Electric/Regent
19	Central/Pavilion/Pullman
20	Cinema/Bijou
★24	Crystal Palace Picture House
26	New Gaiety/Astoria
★27	Rialto/Granada
★29	Albany/Century
31	State/Granada
32	Regal
33	Astoria/Cannon/MGM
35	Rex
36	Odeon
39	Warner/Warner Village/Vue

★adjacent to the borough boundary

Sunday opening was down to seven. Twice in 1930 and once in 1931 (the twelfth application), there was only a one vote majority against.

The cinema owners gained a powerful ally in the Bishop of Croydon who often enjoyed going to the pictures. He was not, however, in favour of the same sort of film being shown on Sunday as on other days and he worked up a scheme supported by the cinema proprietors by which they would open only from 6 p.m. to 11 p.m. on that day, their employees would not have to work more than six consecutive days (and would get a day off in lieu of working on Sunday), and programmes of a 'healthy character' suitable for the Sabbath would be chosen. In 1932, the Sunday Entertainments Act permitted a local referendum on the opening of cinemas on the Sabbath and the first major instance of this occurred in Croydon on Tuesday 29 November 1932, where success or failure would have coloured the response of later referendums. Cinemas erected huge posters urging people to vote in favour. Thousands of helpers with 800 cars were active on polling day when just over half the electorate of 117,160 voted. A crowd of 8,000 people gathered to hear the result declared at 10.30pm: FOR SUNDAY OPENING: 34,617. AGAINST: 24,386. MAJORITY IN FAVOUR: 10,231.

The Croydon Borough Council sanctioned the opening of cinemas on Sunday and it became reality on 12 March 1933 when films were screened to huge audiences from 6 p.m. to 11 p.m. and the proprietors donated seven-and-a-half per cent of the gross to charity. Sunday films were usually old ones, shown for the one day only, and often in poor condition. A special Sunday Film Selection Committee was formed by Croydon Council to view questionable titles.

This committee kept up its work during the Second World War. One unidentified cinema dared to show unauthorised films and the committee sought to suspend its right to open on

Sundays for three months. In the first six months of 1944, when an average of 15,000 people attended the borough's cinemas each Sunday, the committee considered 1,039 titles submitted for showing and arranged to view fifteen of them, rejecting seven as unsuitable for screening on that day. These were: *Confessions* (murder mystery comedy-drama), *The Lodger* (period murder melodrama), *A Man's World* (sabotage drama), *Off the Record* (crooks and newspaper comedy-drama), *'Neath Brooklyn Bridge* (juvenile drama), *Spooks Run Wild* (comedy thriller) and *Phantom Lady* (thriller). One councillor of this period, not on the selection committee, noted that because of the war he could only get to the cinema on Sunday. 'When I do', he complained, 'I see a tremendous lot of utter rubbish and trash, films so ancient that you have to exercise imagination to a quite unreasonable extent to follow the stories. When I asked members of the Committee, I found that they frowned on murder films, but after a week's hard work I regard a good cold-blooded murder as sheer entertainment.'

Sunday opening by this time commenced at 4.30 p.m., after Sunday schools had finished. During the 1950s, the bigger first-run cinemas began showing new films for seven days, beginning on the Sunday. The Sunday Selection Committee still maintained a beady eye on local film fare and was not disbanded until 26 June 1961. As late as 1959, new X certificate horror pictures (even 'respectable' ones like *The Bad Seed)* were replaced by blander fare. Sexy films were also of great interest to the Selection Committee and they banned the Eros from showing *Lady Chatterley's Lover* (a French version released in 1956) on a Sunday.

Film exhibition in Great Britain came to be dominated by three major companies from the 1930s, which were the first to screen all the major new mainstream films through their separate weekly circuit releases. The Gaumont and ABC chains started in the late 1920s. ABC came to be represented in the Borough of Croydon by the Hippodrome and Savoy and by the Rex Norbury and Regal Purley. The Gaumont chain gained a stake in the huge independent Davis Theatre in central Croydon and did not need to acquire or build its own outlet; its weekly programmes also played in later years at smaller circuits' cinemas at Thornton Heath and Purley. The third national chain was Odeon which came to power in the late 1930s and had cinemas in the centre of Croydon and at South Norwood. In later years, the Astoria Purley was also able to access its weekly release.

Most of the remaining, generally smaller, cinemas had to make do with showing the circuit releases later, playing lesser new films and foreign pictures of specialised appeal, or booking reissues. Only the Classic, South Croydon made a virtue out of a repertory policy.

The cinemas that dominate the story of Croydon's cinemas are three in the town centre: the Davis Theatre, the Savoy (later ABC/Cannon/Safari) and the Odeon North End. Increasingly few people remember the Davis, which was a stupendous, but short-lived, building that also functioned as a live venue. Sadly, it was squeezed out of business by industry politics and a real estate boom. The Odeon was a poor building but its central location and access to popular films ensured that it was very well attended for very many years until it, too, fell victim to its site's redevelopment potential. The Savoy was a huge and well designed cinema, second only to the Davis in size, located on the fringe of the town centre, but able to draw on a good number of the top hits.

Cinema building came in three waves. There were those opened before 1914 (when the First World War stopped construction) which were often fine for the time but which generally became fleapits and also rans as larger and more modern cinemas came along; there were the large cinemas built from 1928 until the Second World War again stopped construction. In the 1970s, most of the country's surviving circuit cinemas were split up into two, three or more auditoria to run films longer and offer more choice, and this happened to the ABC and Odeon in Croydon as well as the Astoria Purley, extending the life of these buildings until the arrival of multiplexes in the last twenty years, with the two in the borough eliminating all surviving mainstream competition.

In addition to the cinemas listed in this book, there were at least three instances of proposed cinemas in other areas, as in the 1930s it was considered a matter of commercial necessity for outlying shopping centres to have a cinema. Selsdon had a population of only 5,000 in 1935 but was rapidly expanding. When an application was made to build a 1,000-1,200-seat cinema with car park in Addington Road, permission was refused by Coulsdon and Purley Council. The local Residents Association argued that it would seriously lower the value of adjacent houses. In 1937, however, Selsdon's Chamber of Commerce was so gravely concerned by the loss of business it felt resulted from the lack of a cinema that it informed all the major circuits that there was an excellent site available. Hopes were raised when a representative of one large group visited Selsdon in February 1939. Whatever his conclusions were, the outbreak of war put an end to Selsdon's hopes.

In Addiscombe, which had a modest cinema at the East Croydon end from 1911 to 1917, there were later plans for a purpose-built cinema much further away from the town centre. In 1927, the specially-formed Addiscombe Cinema Co. engaged architects L.W. Griffiths and H.V.M. Emerson to design a cinema in Lower Addiscombe Road to seat 1,200 with a stage and tea room. In January 1937, there were plans for a 1,500-seat cinema on the same road at the junction of Bingham Road and Ashburton Road where now stands the Hamilton Court block of flats (this may well have been the site for the earlier proposal as well). These latest plans were drawn up for H.V. Weingott by a very prominent cinema architect, Cecil Masey, and approved by Croydon Corporation but the scheme was postponed in July. The promoters may have been scared off by the Odeon circuit's interest in building in Addiscombe (on its internal list of active projects in October – site unidentified), or Odeon may have become interested in taking over Weingott's proposal (it took over his cinema scheme in Brighton.) In the outcome, Odeon built a new cinema further out of Croydon, approximately equidistant between Croydon and Bromley, at Elmers End.

Shirley, too, might have had a cinema of its own. In 1936, a picture house was proposed for the corner of Wickham Road and Mead Way, but nearby residents objected and, as the site was meant for houses, the Council would not approve the scheme. A revised application was rejected in October 1937.

This book covers the present Borough of Croydon, even though Purley and Coulsdon formed a separate borough until 1965, and it also includes four cinemas in Upper Norwood, three of which were on the other side of the road from the borough boundary running down the middle of it, as these would have been heavily patronised by people from Croydon.

Allen Eyles
January 2006

one

Central
Croydon

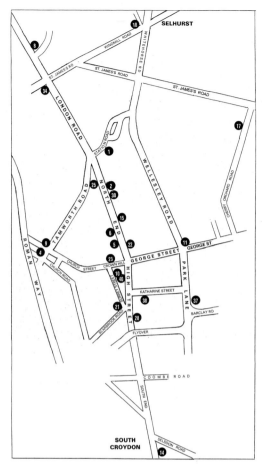

CENTRAL CROYDON

1   Station Picture Hall/King's Picture Hall
2   Electric/Picture House – Picture House/
    Odeon
4   Dome/Olympia
5   Cosie
6   Queen's Hall
8   London Electric Hall/Broad Green
    Cinema/Pavilion
9   Tamworth Hall/Star
10 Bio Picture Lane/Standard/Weekend
    Picture Palace
11 Public Hall
14 Swan Electric/Central Hall/Dome/Savoy/
    Classic
15 Cinematograph Theatre/Palladium
17 Addiscombe Picture Palace
18 Selhurst Picture Palace/Luxor
21 Opheum/Cinema Royal/Palladium
22 Scala
23 Hippodrome – Classic/Oscar/Focus
25 Prince's
28 Davis Theatre
30 Empire/Eros
34 Savoy/ABC/Cannon/Safari
37 Fairfield Halls
38 David Lean
40 Warner Village/Vue

Station Picture Hall/West Croydon Picture Hall/King's Picture Palace, No. 4 Station Buildings, Station Road, West Croydon

Croydon's first cinema opened in May 1908. The entrance was through one of a line of shops which survive to this day (at No. 12 Station Road) and it is occupied in early 2006 by The Edge @ Wax, selling menswear and underground dance music.

Initially offering a half-hour of 'living pictures' for a penny, the Station Picture Hall had 120 seats in a space of 860 sq ft, extending behind the shop to the immediate left. Called the Penny Picture Palace, it attracted praise from the trade paper *Rinking World and Picture Theatre News* in April 1910 for the use of electric light bulbs to draw attention to its frontage: 'For a humble show this is noteworthy ... and unusual'.

Even in 1913, when it was known as the West Croydon Picture Hall, there was no public toilet, only one for staff use. This was not much of a problem, though, until programmes became much longer. The cinema constantly changed hands from 1912 onwards and its name had been altered to the King's Picture Palace by May 1914. Applications for a transfer of licence were made in both July and September 1916. The last licence that seems to have been granted expired on 15 October 1917, and the cinema is therefore thought to have closed by that time.

The Station Picture Hall has become the King's Picture Palace in this October 1916 view across the railway line. The vertical sign at first floor level at the bend in the road reads 'LIVING PICTURES'. See frontispiece for an earlier 1910 closer view. (CTA/Tony Moss Collection.)

Electric Theatre/Picture House, No. 108 North End

The Electric Theatre opened on Saturday 31 July 1909 in the centre of town, built by one of the first cinema circuits in the country, Electric Theatres (1908) Ltd. It had a long, narrow entrance through existing property to an auditorium behind, which was newly built at right angles to the entrance with the far wall meeting a side wall of the Empire Theatre (also set well back behind a narrow entrance on North End).

The Electric began with a change of programme on Monday and Thursday and films showing from 2 p.m. to 11 p.m. A full hour's entertainment was offered for 3d (children: 2d). There was seating for approximately 600 patrons. On the first Monday, the demand was so great that people had to be turned away. A few weeks after opening, a coloured film called *The Life of Christ* was shown, and there is mention of two projectors being used, avoiding breaks for the changing of reels. In a report dated 2 November 1909 by the Metropolitan Police's 'W' division, picking out the best and worst cinemas as requested by the Home Office, this was selected as the best, along with a cinema in Brixton: 'The admission to the two … is 3d and 6d and the persons frequenting them are of good middle class and the exhibitions are of an interesting nature'.

It is unclear why the Electric closed on 1 April 1911, less than two years after opening, for extensive alterations and redecoration. It was said that this would take an appreciable period – and it certainly did. The most frequent reasons for cinemas closing temporarily were financial problems (but the Electric circuit was still doing quite well as a whole) or to enlarge the auditorium – yet, when the Electric opened its doors again on 10 March 1913, it had only

An audience at the Electric in March 1910. They may have been more neatly dressed than usual in anticipation of being photographed by *The Chronicle*. Note the wooden seat backs.

North End, Croydon, in 1910, with the Electric Theatre advertising its presence on the exposed upper side wall to the right. Beyond, half obscured, lies the tall white frontage of the Empire Theatre, later Eros Cinema. (CTA/Tony Moss Collection.)

616 seats. It did, however, undergo a change of name, to Picture House. There are references to new fittings and over 1,000 lamps illuminating the long corridor from North End to the doors of the auditorium. The re-opening programme included the premiere screening of *White Sea Fisheries.*

The Dome/Olympia, No. 11 Lower Church Street

No photographs seem to exist showing this former covered fruit, vegetables and fish market – a conspicuous building with frontages on three streets – after it was converted, around 1909, into a 300-seat cinema called the Dome. It offered continuous shows from 2.30 p.m. to 11 p.m. After being redecorated and re-upholstered in August 1910, it began advertising its programmes in the local press. Special matinees for children were introduced on Saturdays, admission one penny. Dainty teas were served free of charge to patrons from 4 p.m. to 6 p.m. Mondays to Fridays.

In March 1912 the Dome was for sale as a going concern and it continued in business under various proprietors, being renamed the Olympia by February 1916. It closed later that year – perhaps specifically to enable its next use as a barracks, perhaps as a result of problems of staffing and management caused by the First World War.

From 1927 to 1973, the premises became furniture rooms for E. Reeves. They were demolished in 1973 and the site grassed over as part of road improvements.

THE DOME,
LOWER CHURCH STREET, CROYDON.
Croydon's Premier Electric Theatre.
NOW OPEN.
The World's Brightest and Best Coloured Pictures.
CONTINUOUS PERFORMANCES, 2.30 TILL 10.30 P.M.
Prices—3d. & 6d.   Children, 2d.
The Children's Home of Delight and Instruction.

Cosie Picture Palace, No. 31a North End (Hedgis Yard)

A 150-seat cinema with two exits appeared in early December 1909, occupying a triangular space previously used as carriage showrooms in a building alongside Hedgis Yard. In 1971, it was described as having been 'down the side of Kennard's, where the Arcade starts', and in the 1980s was remembered as 'a small room at the end of a passage between Kennard's and a Lyons tea shop.' In *The Post in Croydon* (11 January 1989), Miss B. Rosier recalled: 'In it were shown very jerky "moving pictures". I was taken several times by my grandparents; we sat on "shop chairs" and there were bare boards on the floor. The stars I remember were John Bunny and Flora Finch plus a small white dog who constantly chased John Bunny up and down ladders much to the amusement of the audience who had paid an entrance fee of 1d for children and 2d for adults. The projector was worked by hand and often broke down which meant a long wait in the dark until it was mended'.

At one point this low price cinema was being operated by Edward F. Young, who later also ran the Star in Tamworth Road. The last licensee appears to have been Thomas Windibank of Croydon (who also ran the first cinema at Broad Green for a while). No licence was granted after 1914 and the Cosie had probably closed in 1912.

The late cinema organ expert Tony Moss noted: 'Harry Davidson (born in Croydon in 1892) secured his first job here as pianist for silent movies, from 1910 to 1912. He played early organs in cinemas from 1912 to 1917, when he was appointed musical director to the Tyne Theatre, Newcastle, before opening the Majestic Leeds in 1922 and the Commodore Hammersmith in 1929, his first theatre organ proper. He took over the baton of the Commodore Grand Orchestra from Joseph Muscant in 1933, and became famous for his Old Time Dance Orchestra from 1943, after a short spell as organist at the Ritz Oxford'.

The Cosie was later Riley's billiard hall, but Hedgis Yard and the former Kennard's department store have disappeared in the massive Debenhams/Centrale Drummond Centre redevelopment of this part of North End.

Queen's Hall, No. 57 North End

Opened on Monday 27 December 1909, this was a reconstruction of existing premises to the plans of architect Ernest Bates. It was named after the Queen's Hall, Peter Street, Bristol, which was operated by the same proprietor. The Croydon hall had a sloping floor, plush red tip-up seats, and a colour scheme of red and green 'in the Georgian style'. Orchestra stalls were 6d, other seats 3d. It was the first of Croydon's cinemas to have a uniformed attendant outside. This venue had closed by 1912 when there was a glut of cinematograph theatres in the centre of Croydon. No photographs have been located. The building later housed an auction mart, Dorothy Perkins and the SOS Staff Bureau but has been a branch of the Woolwich Building Society for many years.

London Electric Hall/Broad Green Cinema/Pavilion, Nos 204-210 (later No. 378) London Road

Built outside the centre of Croydon on the busy London Road at Broad Green, the London Electric Hall opened on Saturday 26 March 1910. The auditorium was built at an oblique angle to the main road, directly behind the offices and yard occupying at the corner of London Road and Bensham Lane. An entrance with a pitched glass roof extended from London Road to the back to the auditorium, with the projection box at first floor level. A paybox was set into the right-hand wall of the entrance passage.

The cinema claimed 400 seats (no balcony) and had a very low admission price of 2d (with reserved seats costing a penny more). The short films on the opening programme were supplemented by specially shot scenes of bustling Croydon to encourage attendance – patrons were rewarded if they spotted themselves, the top prize being £2.

In July 1910, the cinema was taken over by Thomas Windibank, who also ran the Cosie. He introduced family discounts at matinees and employed twelve musicians to accompany the films on Tuesday evenings. Around 1921 the cinema was operated by Dellow & Co. and was redecorated and re-seated. In April 1922, it was offered for sale with eight years left on the lease. It was acquired and managed by W.S. Pinney who renamed it the Broad Green Cinema. By 1926 it had become the Pavilion, leased by R.O. Baker.

Rose Dawson of New Addington remembered going with her parents every Saturday night in the late 1920s: 'There was quite a friendly atmosphere there. When we went up a few steps and paid to go in, we could obtain a raffle ticket. In the interval we had a sing-song – the song sheet was shown on the screen. Then the raffle was drawn, the prize generally being of groceries and fruit. Besides the news and features, there was always a serial which I, as a child, used to follow with avid interest and look forward to the following Saturday. It was always a cliffhanger, sometimes quite literally, with cowboys, villains, heroines in dire peril. The film used to break quite often and there would be comments from the audience while it was being repaired. Also some joker would occasionally pass some comment during the film and there would be general laughter amongst the audience'.

The owner, Mr Baker, applied in January 1931 to fit two pairs of swing doors to keep out the draught and improve the appearance of the entrance. Business must have been badly affected by the opening almost opposite in March 1936 of the huge and luxurious Savoy as both offered cheap seats at 6d and the Pavilion's top price of 1s 3d was only three pence less than the top price on weekdays for sitting in the front circle at the Savoy. For virtually the same price, one could watch major new pictures instead of the old ones at the Pavilion, but it probably seemed friendlier and cosier to some of its patrons. It now had 302 seats on one floor. It remained open under a further owner,

R. Dormer, until around the outbreak of the Second World War. It then became the Tudor dance hall, but has long been demolished, the whole area being turned over to fenced-in parking space.

Tamworth Hall/Star, No. 47 Tamworth Road

The building was erected by the Christian Mission (which became the Salvation Army) and opened in 1873 as their ninth centre, the very first outside the East End of London. It was vacated by the Salvationists in 1887 and as the Tamworth Hall seems to have become a cinema from early 1910. It was certainly licensed in May of that year. There was seating for 175 people in 1,368 sq ft of space.

It underwent a period of closure, being re-opened in March 1912 by Edward F. Young (who also ran the Cosie). He renamed it the Star after adding a new vestibule, redecorating and refitting the interior, and raising the accommodation to 250 seats (though children were known to sit on the wide window sills when all the seats were taken). Its last licence expired on 15 October 1917, so it must have closed prior to that time, another failure of the First World War period. During its short life as a cinema, it was operated by at least four proprietors.

It was later used for storing cars. Demolition in the area for new roads and open spaces (which claimed the site of the nearby Dome/Olympia) took away the buildings to one side, but it still stands in 2005, currently in use as the Jiyu Seishin Bujutsu Centre or Free Spirit Martial Arts Centre and Gym.

Bio Picture Land/Standard/New Standard Picture Playhouse/Weekend Picture Palace, No. 39-40 Surrey Street (Market Hall)

A licence was issued to William Buxton to run a cinema in part of the Market Hall. Opened around May 1910 as the Bio Picture Land, it provided no seats, so audiences had to stand. In the previously mentioned police survey of November 1909, this cinema was picked out as one of three of 'the worst type' (the other examples being in Brixton and Clapham): 'The admission … is 1d and the surroundings and persons frequenting the place are poor.' Clearly the low price attracted a rough element. However, the superintendent signing the report noted that the police took no exception to the films being shown.

In 1910, a film fire brought about temporary closure. When it re-opened on Monday 20 March 1911, a new projection box with a Tyler-Erneman flickerless projector had been set up outside the auditorium and 300 plush-covered seats had been installed. There were matinees from 2 p.m. to 5 p.m. and evening shows from 6 p.m. to 10.30 p.m. Then, or soon after, it was renamed the Standard.

In a 1971 letter to the *Croydon Advertiser,* Samuel Roberts recalled: 'Back in 1911, my sweetheart gave me her penny and I provided the other penny, thus we were all set to go to the Standard in Surrey Street. What exciting programmes we saw! There was a large space in front of the seats and up to the screen and if all the seats were full we used to sit on the floor, about 100 of us.'

The cinema defied the ban on Sunday opening described in the introduction to this book and even advertised the fact in 1914. The licensee was brought to court but continued flouting the law until he was fined £5 and costs for having opened on 5 July and 12 August of that year. When it became clear that the licence would not be renewed until a new proprietor took over, the lease passed to Arthur P. Brooks who ran it as the New Standard Picture Playhouse, showing some of the oldest films then available.

However, it was known as the Weekend by the end of 1918 when it had obtained permission to be the only cinema officially open on the Sabbath. It followed the odd practice of opening only on Saturday and Sunday from 2.30 p.m. to 10.30 p.m. – perhaps the space was used by the Market Hall during the week? However, when Mrs Kate Lilian Schulman bought the business from Brooks, retaining him as manager with day-to-day control, she opened from Monday to Saturday, beginning Easter Monday 1920, following thorough renovation and redecoration at a cost of £1,000, including new heating equipment, curtains, and illuminated statuary around the screen. There were now 350 seats with standing room for 100. Two projectors were used, with a 74ft throw to the screen. The musical accompaniment was provided by a Professor Kemp who could handle several instruments including piano, organ, violin and cello. At one point, he planned to play for more than 82 hours continuously to beat a record set in Germany and win £10,000 offered as a prize by Consolidated Music of Chicago. The new opening policy was a flop and the place reverted to operating only on Saturdays and Sundays from Christmas Day 1920 (a Saturday) as the Weekend Picture Palace. Even this did not work out and the cinema had closed by 1923.

The site of the Market Hall is now part of the new Grants development with the Vue multiplex above.

The Public Hall. East Croydon station is in the distance to the right. Like the Public Hall, the building with the clock tower has long ago disappeared. (John Gent Collection.)

Public Hall, George Street (northeast corner of the junction of Wellesley Road)

The Public Hall was no stranger to film shows when it became a full-time cinema from Whit Monday 16 May 1910. Gale and Polden's Animated Pictures had played here in August 1906, for example, and Ernest Mansell with Gale and Polden presented seasons of 'animated pictures' in August and December 1908. It offered 531 seats on the main floor and 116 in the balcony, where the projection box was established at the rear.

In August 1909, Mansell showed programmes for at least five weeks with an orchestra, titles including *Life in the Army and Navy* and *The Reedham Orphanage Boys at Drill*. This season seems to have prompted the Public Hall to become a full-time cinema from Whit Monday 1910. It was quite large for such a purpose, now seating 700. Programmes included items of local interest like *Junior Whitgift School Sports*.

Press advertising ceased in mid-June but this is not proof of closure (as later, many cinemas advertised only intermittently, or not at all). However, it seems clear that full-time cinema use ceased by the end of 1910 although the building was licensed to show films until 1920 and probably continued to do so on an occasional hire basis.

In March 1938, there was a proposal noted in the film trade press to build a new cinema at one corner of George Street and Wellesley Road. Providing a conveniently large space, the Public Hall might well have been the site in mind. In any event, road widening for an underpass has consumed most or all of the space it occupied, the new north-east corner being occupied by a modern parade of shops with a Barclays Bank in the centre.

The tall frontage of the Dome South Croydon, topped by a cupola, is behind the garage sign and before the church in this view taken on 31 March 1927 with part of the Swan and Sugar Loaf public house at left. (John Gent Collection.)

Swan Electric Theatre/Central Hall/Dome/Savoy/Classic/Tatler/Classic, No. 3 Brighton Road, South Croydon

Taking its name from the nearby Swan and Sugar Loaf hotel and public house, the Swan Electric Theatre was opened on Saturday 26 November 1910 by the Lunn Cinematograph Co., specially formed for the purpose with capital being raised locally. The narrow frontage had ornate decoration at a lower level with a cupola or dome on top. There were some 500 seats on the site, which was 2,194 sq ft.

Although it served the population living on the southern side of the town, it was readily accessible by public transport from farther afield: corporation trams could bring patrons from as far as Thornton Heath for a penny. (This advantage always remained: in its later years as a Classic, several bus routes would drop patrons coming from further north at the entrance doors.)

The Swan Electric also tried to win patronage by boasting of the longest programme in town with at least twelve films in each show (this was, of course, before pictures became feature-length). Yet the cinema quickly closed, to re-open under new management on Thursday 6 April 1911. By October 1911 it had been taken over by the James Watt circuit and renamed the Central Hall after other cinemas in the group (including one at South Norwood). A small balcony seating 150 was added. By 1916 the name had been mounted on both sides of the cupola to be seen from a distance in either direction.

In 1927 the Central Hall was renamed the Dome. It closed around the time that talkies arrived and re-opened in 1932 as the Savoy, only to close again in 1933 when it was said to have had ten different proprietors over the past five years and to have been closed for two of those years.

Its future seemed bleak. But then it was acquired by Sam Seeman, who brought in an architect, Norman Evans, to modernise the place. Six weeks of reconstruction followed before it re-opened on Monday 3 September 1934, and this presumably was when the dome went from the frontage. Seeman had pioneered the idea of presenting high quality, low-priced repertory programmes the previous year at Notting Hill Gate, London. He formed a new company, Unique Cinema (Croydon) Ltd, and apparently launched a competition to find a new name. The highly suitable final choice was Classic and the cinema actually boasted about showing old films. The first presentation was of *Viennese Nights* plus the Disney cartoon *Three Little Pigs*, the first in perfected Technicolor. Prices of admission were 6d in the afternoon, and 9d and 1s in the evening. As the shows were usually only two hours long, this permitted two performances in the evening.

The name and policy were so successful that a whole circuit of Classic repertory cinemas sprang up, including a purpose-built cinema in Baker Street, central London. For some thirty years the South Croydon outlet paid its way, benefiting from the absence of rival cinemas in the immediate vicinity, although it was not as big a moneymaker as some of the other Classics. It had a very cramped entrance foyer, a minute balcony, and one of the smallest projection rooms anywhere. But it was shrewdly programmed, widely advertised and well maintained so that it avoided the rundown look and fleapit status of most cinemas playing old films.

Left: The Classic South Croydon in the 1960s. The end of a poster frame, where notable forthcoming attractions were publicised, can be seen at upper left.

Above: A poor quality view of the Classic South Croydon's auditorium from the small straight-fronted balcony, the front edge of which largely obscures the door to the manager's office in the left hand side wall of the stalls. The light from the office could be a distraction during performances. (CTA/Tony Moss Collection.)

A ban on smoking on Mondays and Fridays was introduced in August 1957, gaining massive publicity in the national press (main story on the front page of *The Daily Mirror*, no less), but the experiment had to be called off the following January. There was another experiment from Monday 2 March 1959, of calling the cinema the Classic Continental and concentrating on foreign films. Subtitled pictures had often been shown before but an exclusive diet soon affected attendances and the cinema reverted to ordinary programming as the Classic a few months later. Such well-promoted policy changes always had some benefit of drawing attention to the cinema, and usually enjoyed an initial success. The Classic actually did remarkably well for a while after its Continental phase, as though patrons were registering their delight at having it back as before.

In 1962, a modernisation scheme (reported as costing £10,000) was carried out that included enlargement of the projection room. The auditorium was by now rather plain – long and straight-sided with no interesting decorative features. The Classic never closed during the improvements, which were completed on 21 September 1962.

By 1970, admissions were clearly faltering as, from 4 October of that year, the circuit turned the Classic into one of its Tatler club cinemas showing uncensored sex films and featuring live strippers – supported principally by elderly patrons. This was a rather surprising change as most Tatlers were in seedy working class areas. There were some Saturday late night shows of ordinary films open to the general public. The cinema became the Classic again with public performances in August 1971 when a Classic executive admitted the 'adult' film policy had been a mistake for the area (although Tatler shows continued on Sunday afternoons until 17 December 1972). One problem was that the expected degree of church opposition had not taken place to provide enough free publicity for the launch!

When the new three-screen Classic opened in central Croydon in 1972, the future of the old Classic became doubtful. The curtains closed for the last time at 10.18pm on Saturday 22 September 1973 as a revival screening of *The Wild Bunch* came to an end. The building remained vacant for several years until it was given a new Tudoresque decor as a nightclub/restaurant called Scot's Dine and Dance. Only the flat ceiling with art deco circular plasterwork from the 1930s that once surrounded a central light fitting was recognisable from its cinema past. Extending its long history as a place for a night out, in 2006 it is the home of Up the Creek Too! Comedy Cabaret Club or just The Comedy Club (conflicting signs are on display).

Cinematograph Theatre/Palladium, Nos 62-64 North End

Opening on Wednesday 21 December 1910, this was an addition to the Pyke Circuit, a rapidly expanding London-area chain headed by the ambitious entrepreneur Montagu A. Pyke. It followed ten others at Edgware Road, Finsbury Park, Walham Green, Ealing, Oxford Street, Shepherds Bush, Piccadilly Circus, Hammersmith, Clapham Junction and Walworth. The Croydon venture was one of those grouped under Amalgamated Cinematograph Theatres Ltd.

The new building replaced the premises of a firm of solicitors and an old-world garden at the rear. The frontage was set back from adjacent property as part of the long-term plan to widen the road. Construction took less than three months and a new cinema seating 800 on one floor resulted. It had a mahogany paybox open to the street and a 128ft-long vestibule leading to an auditorium which, being 112ft long by 50ft wide, was actually shorter in length and only slightly wider than the approach to it. The auditorium ran straight back (rather than being set at right angles to the entrance passage), with the far outside wall facing the northern corner of the Whitgift Grammar School cricket ground.

Croydon's Cinematograph Theatre with banner advertising a special programme for the week commencing Monday 22 March 1915: a film and slide lecture 'as presented to the King and Queen' with three separate performances daily at 3 p.m., 6 p.m. and 9 p.m., 200 seats at one shilling, 300 at 6d and 200 at 3d. (National Monuments Record.) The cinema was entered through the doors to the right of the paybox which may be just visible under the word ANTARCTIC on the banner. Note the monogram PC for Pyke Circuit on the pilasters to each side of the entrance. By 1928, a large poster advertising the current programme replaced the assortment of smaller ones on the side wall of the adjacent property which was then awaiting demolition. The frontage above ground floor level is clearly recognisable in 2006.

Like other Pyke picture houses, it was built and fitted to a high standard for that time, with luxurious carpeting and seats. 'What a feeling of richness one had on entering that wide entrance, stepping up the wide carpeted grand staircase which led to the plush foyer with its potted plants and palms,' recalled a former patron, Frank Shonfeld, in a letter to the *Croydon Advertiser* in 1971. Although it had seats at 3d and 6d, its top price of 1s was twice that asked by competitors. There were two projectors and a screen 18ft wide. There was a curtained-off area for the musicians who accompanied the silent films. The cinema also had a straight 2-manual organ.

The Pyke circuit ran into financial difficulties after 1913. Pyke was sacked from his job as managing director. On Sundays at this period (when cinemas were not licensed to open), the hall was used for meetings of the North End Brotherhood.

A new management took over later in 1915 and renamed the cinema the Palladium. It was leased in the 1920s by a company called Croydon Amusements which also ran the Hippodrome in Crown Hill. A notable attraction at the Palladium was Chaplin's *The Circus* which was shown in October 1928 and attracted 3,507 patrons on a Saturday.

Sound apparatus was installed at the Palladium six months after the Hippodrome and the inaugural feature was the same at both houses, Al Jolson's *The Singing Fool*. It opened at the Palladium on 12 August 1929 with special rows of seats with headphones for the deaf. The Palladium often played the same programme as the Hippodrome and the two halls shared a single copy of the newsreel which was ferried back and forth.

It is very surprising that, less than a year after installing sound, the Palladium closed for good, having been bought by Woolworth's to expand their store next door. Of course, the Hippodrome was the more important of the two cinemas with a much larger capacity, and Woolworths may have made an irresistible offer. The last day of operation was Saturday 10 May 1930 and the final attraction was *The Locked Door* with Barbara Stanwyck. The organ is believed to have been transferred to the restaurant of Kennard's store across the road. The Palladium name was almost immediately adopted by the Cinema Royal in Surrey Street.

In 2006, the area that the original Palladium occupied is still part of Woolworth's.

Above and below: The long entrance hall (looking towards the entrance) and the auditorium of the Croydon Cinematograph Theatre. The screen is left bare (concealment by curtains was not yet the custom).

Addiscombe Picture Palace, No. 131 Cherry Orchard Road, Addiscombe

Even this very small cinema, seating only 132, occupying 828 sq ft, and serving a local neighbourhood, was launched with display advertisements in the Croydon press as a 'high class picture theatre … all the latest subjects depicted by the most perfect machine yet put on the market. Absolutely no flicker'. It attempted to draw from a wider area – 'Two minutes from East Croydon Station. Trams from all parts outside' – but it would have needed a fast tram to get you there that quickly. At the same time, it emphasised a low single admission price of 2d.

The cinema opened on Wednesday 8 February 1911 at 3 p.m. Shows were continuous from 3 p.m. to 10.30 p.m. with children admitted Saturday afternoons at half price. It was not licensed after 1917 and must have closed during that year if not before. Some of its patronage may have been lost to the skating rink which opened up in the same road.

It may have been a conversion of retail premises. It certainly became that. After being Jackson's Shoe Shop, it was divided into two, and in 2005 the occupants of No. 131 are The TV Shop. It is hard to believe there was ever a cinema there. The old projection box was situated over the side passage to the right.

Selhurst Picture Palace/Luxor, corner of Windmill Road and Hampton Road, Selhurst

The Selhurst Picture Palace Ltd was a company formed to take a 99-year lease on a site 60ft-long on Windmill Road and 110ft long on Hampton Road from 25 December 1910 with an option to purchase the freehold. Plans were drawn up by Westminster architect J.J. Taylor for a cinema 60ft by 48ft to cost £2,500 to construct. Shares were offered for sale in the *Croydon Chronicle* in January 1911. It was emphasised that the site, well to the north of the town centre, lay at an important junction crossed by electric trams from Crystal Palace, Penge, Anerley, South Norwood and Croydon, and that there was a large working-class population from which to draw.

Financial support was evidently forthcoming as the Selhurst Picture Palace was built and opened three months later, on Saturday 15 April 1911, with 504 seats. Programmes were continuous from 2.30 p.m. to 10.30 p.m. (special children's matinees were introduced on

The Selhurst Picture Palace in 1911. (John Gent Collection – CTA/Tony Moss Collection.)

Saturdays from 29 April 1911). Prices of admission were 3d and 6d (reduced to 3d and 2d for children under 12).

The building was closed by fire in 1913. It had re-opened by 1920. Programmes were changed two or three times a week and there was an orchestra of three accompanying the silent films in the mid-1920s.

The cinema was renamed the Luxor in the early 1930s. It re-opened on 28 January 1937 after a period of closure for reasons that remain obscure. In a 1994 letter, Julian F. Alderton noted: 'An uncle of mine, Frank Bartlett, was a joint owner in the 1930s when he was also employed as a representative by Paramount Films. Frank bought the Luxor with two partners, Percy Holland and Edward Vicary, both of whom lived in north London. The previous owner was Leslie Murray and I believe he only showed silent films there. Frank Bartlett eventually sold his share to his partners. I was occasionally taken there as a child and I clearly remember visiting the projection room during performances and being quite terrified at having to walk past the mercury arc rectifier to get there – I was quite convinced that it was in imminent danger of exploding! The Luxor was certainly a fleapit. My brother and I were strictly forbidden by our parents from visiting the Luxor unaccompanied, a rule which we blatantly disregarded. I remember my uncle commenting that once or twice each year the seats in the front two rows had to be replaced, for reasons which require little elaboration. My final memory, and this is open to doubt, is that the partners employed a manager at the time whose name was Mr Micklejohn or Michaeljohn'.

Although the cinema played films long after their debut in the centre of Croydon, it was far enough away and well enough positioned to hold its own until the war years. This was the only one of the Borough's cinemas to be permanently closed by enemy action during Second World War, as recalled in a 1990 letter by Croydon resident H.F. Hartwell: 'The V1 flying bombs did extensive damage as they exploded on the surface of the ground, the blast going out in all directions (2,000 lbs. of it). One of them came in from the south east on Saturday 1 July 1944 at approximately 10.15 p.m. and completely destroyed the Gloucester public house [on the other side of Windmill Road from the Luxor, on the corner of Whitehorse Road] and the best part of a row of shops, Nos 89 to 109 Whitehorse Road. It also destroyed part of the Public Baths building [in Windmill Road]. The Luxor Cinema was badly damaged. I assume that the V1 fell behind the row of shops near the Gloucester, so that the blast had no obstruction as there was only an open timber yard across the road, next to the Luxor'.

The building was torn down and the ground cleared around 1950. Its site was later used by the Bingham Motor Co. as an outdoor area to display cars for sale. In 2005, Halfords occupy the site with a car park in front.

Orpheum / Cinema Royal / Palladium, No. 1 Surrey Street (corner of Scarbrook Road)

This was the most conspicuous of central Croydon's early cinemas, occupying a corner site at the top end of Surrey Street (the Hippodrome was at the bottom end). Opening on Monday 23 March 1914, the Orpheum was designed by an architect specialising in cinemas, Gilbert Booth, and seated 680 people with a balcony and boxes. It was built at a cost of £12,500 by a specially formed company whose chairman was Baron von Horst (later interned during the First World War). The downward slope of the land was helpful in providing a rake to the stalls floor. Prices of admission were 1s (for the boxes), 6d and 3d (children half price).

The opening programme, for the first half of the week, was a selection of short films: the English premiere of the American Bison Company's drama *In The Wilds of Africa,* Thanhouser's *The Problem of Love Solved,* several comedies (Essanay's *Hello Trouble,* Keystone's *Cohen Saves the Flag,* Kalem's *A Joke on Jane),* and the Pathé Animated Gazette newsreel. Sound effects were sometimes added to the usual orchestral accompaniment. There was a tea room at the back of the balcony with an open verandah over the corner entrance.

The cinema closed in mid-July 1924, ostensibly 'for cleaning and redecoration'. But clearly more was involved as it did not re-open until 2 p.m. on Monday 23 February 1925 when it became the Cinema Royal under a new proprietor, E.H. Thompson. The first attraction was Huguette Duflos of the Comédie Française in *Konigsmark*. Prices now ranged from 6d to 2s 4d.

In May 1930 the cinema closed for a week, during which it was redecorated and renovated while Western Electric sound equipment was installed. It re-opened on 26 May as the Palladium – in advertising as the 'New Palladium' (the previous Palladium having closed two weeks earlier) – and the '100%-talking' attraction was *Isle of Lost Ships.* In 1942, it advertised itself as 'Croydon's Repertory Cinema', a title the Classic might have disputed, but it was soon back to showing minor new releases, early re-runs and national reissues.

It was leased by Mrs M.H. Dawes and linked with the Connaught Edgware Road. Its seating capacity in the 1940s was 659. Prices ranged from 10d to 1s 9d, considerably undercutting the Davis Theatre almost opposite (where the range was from 1s to 4s 6d).

In 1949 the Palladium was closed for two weeks and redecorated with the exterior repainted light cream. Inside, fluorescent lighting was introduced in red, green and blue tubes (operated, it was claimed, for the first time in any British cinema by dimmers).

Occasionally a brand new Gaumont release programme came the Palladium's way if it couldn't play at the Davis or Hippodrome, but the cinema slowly degenerated into something of a fleapit, not helped by the open-air market which occupied Surrey Street. To the author of this book, it was rather dirty and unwelcoming on occasional visits in the mid-1950s but the image on the screen was bright and well focused and it seemed well attended. It closed on Saturday 25 August 1956 with a booking of *Charley Moon* starring Max Bygraves, supported by *Double Cross,* preceding the demise of the Hippodrome by only two months. It was probably still profitable, thanks to its excellent position, and an early example of a cinema being sold for its site value. It went to Myton Ltd (part of Taylor Woodrow) for 'a very high figure', being demolished in October 1956 to make way for the six-storey block of offices and shops called Surrey House which still stands on the site in 2006.

The imposing frontage of the Orpheum (later Palladium) just prior to opening in 1914.

The Orpheum in the late 1920s when it was briefly known as the Cinema Royal. (John Gent Collection.)

The Palladium, ex-Orpheum/Cinema Royal, in its last week of operation. (Croydon Public Libraries.)

The dome of the Scala can be seen at right – this disappeared when the frontage was rebuilt as Allders extended around it. On the left can be seen the North End Hall which had some special film shows. (John Gent collection.)

Scala, Nos 16-18 North End

The Scala was built next to Allders store to plans of J. W. Stanley Burmester, an architect based in Westminster. It made its debut on Tuesday 22 December 1914 with 882 seats (including 200 in a balcony). There was an 85ft throw from projectors to screen. The side walls of the auditorium, above an oak-panelled dado, were decorated by a French artist with tapestries representing eight different sporting scenes.

From the first, the lights were dimmed and raised instead of being switched on and off as seems to have been the general practice. All the staff were stated to be completely ineligible for military service in the First World War and the proceeds from the opening show were donated to relieve war distress (staffing became a serious problem as war went on, even causing the closure of some picture houses).

Prices of admission in 1914 were 3d and 6d downstairs, and 9d and 1s for the balcony. The first proprietor was Edgar Samuel of Birmingham. Within four years it was being run by Gaiety Picture House (Southampton) Ltd. Advertising boasted: 'Luxurious seats with arms in every part of the house'. Around 1920, according to Tony Moss, a straight organ by William Hill & Son, Norman & Beard Ltd was installed – it had 11 speaking stops on one manual only. It was at the Scala in 1921 that thirteen-year-old schoolboy David Lean paid his first-ever visit to a cinema, catching the latest version of *The Hound of the Baskervilles*. As Lean's biographer, Kevin Brownlow, commented: 'Seen today, the production is a workmanlike telling of Conan Doyle's famous story … but for a boy who had never before seen a moving picture, it was unforgettable.'

The Scala entrance in the mid-1930s after Allders department store extended around it. Its position can be pinpointed today by reference to the round columns above. (*Croydon Advertiser.*)

During the 1920s, Allders store was reconstructed around the Scala and its entrance. A side exit opened onto the store's arcade, from where the Scala's projectors could be heard whirring.

The Scala switched to sound from Monday 16 September 1929, a few weeks after the Davis, Picture House and Palladium. Its lowly position in the booking order is nicely indicated by its first all-talking attraction, *The Doctor's Secret,* having already been shown at the Picture House. There were occasional first-runs but not of releases that any other cinema wanted. It boasted of being 'Croydon's Best Sound Cinema', a slogan that persisted in its press advertising into the 1950s when it had become thoroughly meaningless – not that it can have meant much in the first place.

While the Scala was in an admirable position to attract passing custom, its extremely weak booking position became an increasing handicap. Its occasional first-run programmes continued to be so feeble that only the least discriminating cinemagoers would have been attracted. The atmosphere also became uninviting – a former member of staff remembered rats and mice scuttling about. The Gaiety company was still the operator when it abruptly closed on Sunday 2 March 1952 after a one-day revival of *Monte Cristo's Revenge* plus *The Lady from Tangier.* (The last main booking had been a six-day run to the night before of the Randolph Scott western *Sugarfoot* plus *Girls Never Tell.*) Twenty staff were put out of work.

This was the first of Croydon's cinemas to shut down after the war, and closure seems to have been a last-minute decision. The proprietors claimed that the lease had expired while Allders, which owned the freehold, said that although they had expressed an interest in taking over the space some time before, the Scala's end had come as a surprise. At any rate, Allders soon expanded into the area formerly occupied by the cinema and no trace of it remains today.

Above left: The Croydon Hippodrome advertises an all-talking double bill in 1931.

Above right: In late October 1949, photographed to assess what work was needed when post-war restrictions on repairs were lifted. (CTA/Tony Moss Collection.)

Hippodrome, Crown Hill

The Hippodrome had opened to the public on Monday 1 August 1910, designed by the eminent theatre architects Frank Matcham & Co. for Moss Empires as a 1,500-seat variety theatre replacing the old Theatre Royal on the same site (which had shown some early films, as noted in the Introduction). This had been acquired by Moss Empires in 1909 and renamed the Hippodrome at the same time as an announcement was made that it would be entirely rebuilt as an up-to-date theatre of varieties.

The new Hippodrome was given a big send-off at a private reception for the town's elite hosted by company head Oswald Stoll on the Thursday before the public opening. From the beginning, films from American Bioscope made up one part of the bill, and in July 1911 scenes of the Coronation procession and tour of south London streets were shown.

It was in the spring of 1918 that the Hippodrome went over entirely to films, leaving music hall to the Empire in North End. As a cinema it seated 1,250 and was operated by Croydon Amusements who also ran the first Palladium in North End. The Hippodrome offered full three hour programmes with orchestra – boxes (to seat four) were 8s 6d; the grand circle was 1s 3d; the stalls were 1s or 6d; the fauteuils were 5d; and the upper circle was 3d.

The Hippodrome's finest hour came in 1929 when it was the first London-area cinema outside the West End to obtain the new Vitaphone system for talking pictures, which used ten-minute reels synchronised with sound discs (played on a turntable from the centre outwards). An electrician was specially flown in from Germany to supervise the installation which began on a Friday night and concluded at midnight on Sunday, the cinema opening with Al Jolson in *The Singing Fool* the next day, Monday 4 February. According to trade press advertising by the distributor, the film drew 19,017 paying customers in its first week, with long queues for many of the six performances daily. It ran for three weeks, then returned for a further two weeks from 1 April (when it was screened five times a day).

Other talking features with variety shorts followed, often running two weeks, and the original part-talking picture, *The Jazz Singer,* arrived on 6 May. For six golden months the Hippodrome had the only talking pictures in town. The orchestra which had accompanied silent films was disbanded. When the Palladium was also equipped with sound, the two theatres generally played the same programme despite being only a few minutes' walk apart.

The fast expanding Associated British Cinemas circuit leased the Hippodrome from 2 February 1931 to gain its first outlet in the town. ABC then opened the huge Savoy at Broad Green in 1936. The two cinemas were two-thirds of a mile apart and the main feature of each weekly ABC circuit release was usually shown at both halls (although the supporting film would often vary). The Hippodrome had the great advantage of a central position, attracting walk-in trade from shoppers visiting Croydon (particularly those using the Surrey Street market) whereas the Savoy required more of an effort to be reached by most patrons.

ABC programming ended on Saturday 18 April 1942 and the Hippodrome's lease was taken over by the rival Odeon circuit which, of course, already had a cinema a short distance away in North End, and re-opened the Hippodrome on Monday 4 May. Although the advertised policy was to show revivals ('Films you cannot see at the Odeon you can see here'), after only a couple of weeks the Hippodrome began showing the same weekly circuit release programme as the Odeon for most of the time. This compensated for the rather low seating capacity of the Odeon on its own. The Hippodrome freehold was bought by Odeon in January 1946.

As a cinema, the Hippodrome came to have a rather cold, uninviting atmosphere. Like many other lofty variety theatres, it did not provide an ideal atmosphere for cinemagoing and seemed distinctly old-fashioned. Even in the 1950s, when attendances were declining, the Odeon and Hippodrome still frequently showed the same film, especially if it was a British picture from the cinemas' parent company, the Rank Organisation, which helped the Hippodrome meet its quota obligations and maximised earnings within the company. However, the Hippodrome also showed reissues (like the Jane Russell film *The Outlaw*), 'floating' new releases, some subtitled foreign-language films, and it usually presented the weekly Gaumont release when the Davis Theatre was unavailable.

Although the Hippodrome had priority over other central Croydon cinemas after the Savoy, Davis and Odeon, the pickings were thin. The foyer was modernised shortly before it became one of fifty-nine cinemas Rank closed in late 1956 and early 1957. The Hippodrome's last ever show, on Saturday 3 November 1956, was the Gaumont release of the week, *Run for the Sun,* supported by *Rebel in Town*.

The staff of thirty – including C.W. Bentley, chief of staff, who had been there since 1925 – were offered other jobs with the Odeon circuit. The building had already been sold to British Home Stores to extend its premises. While the front was retained (but altered out of all recognition), the rest of the building was demolished and the BHS extension erected to designs of George Coles & Partners, a firm well known for designing cinemas. In 1972 the structure was converted to a leisure complex incorporating three small cinemas for the Classic circuit.

The imposing entrance to the Prince's Picture House, taken from the cover of a programme in the CTA Archive. The dome remains to this day but the lower entrance area has lost all its exotic detailing as just another shop.

Prince's Picture House, No. 127 North End

The auditorium occupied the former drill hall of the Surrey Yeomanry which had also served as its headquarters. This stretched between Church Path, a narrow footpath running diagonally off North End, and Tamworth Road. The specially formed Croydon Picture House Co. told potential investors that a huge population of 200,000 people was inadequately served by the 5,000 seats at Croydon's existing cinemas (those in the town itself, not the Borough), so the conversion of the hall into a cinema had excellent prospects. Behind the scheme was H.W. Wright who had other cinema interests at Brixton, Nottingham (The Meadows and the New Empress) and Edinburgh (the Elm Row Palace).

In order to attract patrons into the hall from North End, the main shopping thoroughfare, an entrance was established through existing premises there, opposite the Picture House. To make up for its narrowness (16ft wide), a highly ornate Oriental frontage was added, topped by a huge, squat, onion-shaped dome. Patrons purchased tickets, walked through a long foyer, descending some steps, before crossing the public passage of Church Path (roofed over at this point) to enter the auditorium itself.

The architect for the cinema company was H. Berney of Berney & Son, Nos 33 and 35 High Street, Croydon, who was noted as being a member of the parish church and so perhaps responsible for the Vicar of Croydon, W.P.G. McCormick, performing the opening ceremony on the Monday afternoon of 27 June 1921 (he took the opportunity to voice his opposition to Sunday opening).

The long, narrow auditorium was scheduled to seat 1,116 including a balcony at the rear. There were shutters along one side that were opened to ventilate the auditorium between performances. The cinema started off with a symphony orchestra of twelve musicians accompanying the film in both afternoons and evenings. The very first show featured *Three Men in a Boat, Across India with the Duke of Connaught*, plus *Around the Town* and the Pathé Gazette newsreel. The screen was difficult to see from some seats and it had to be brought further forward. This was among 'drastic alterations' advertised in November 1923 when the seating capacity was reduced to 825.

In April 1927, a new company, Prince's (Croydon) Ltd, was registered to take over the cinema with a capital of £3,100. It was headed by Horace Andrews, a pioneer exhibitor (Andrews Pictures). Programming relied heavily on foreign films, particularly Russian, as these were the best the proprietors could obtain (they lacked well-known stars but, being silent, were easily understood with English titles).

Takings for the first year, 1928, amounted to £12,161, with an operating profit of £2,812 and an overall loss of £3,962. The Prince's survived for another year, closing on Saturday 11 May 1929 after a week's run of the double bill *What Do You Know of Love?* starring Stewart Rome plus *The Way of a Transgressor* starring Dorothy Mackaill. An advertised exclusive British premiere run from 20 May of a new Russian historical drama called *Ivan the Terrible* never took place. The owning company went into voluntary liquidation with liabilities of £5,300.

The freehold with vacant possession was offered at auction on Tuesday 30 July. On 27 August, the contents were auctioned: 400 yards of lino, carpet, a heavy curtain, 168 mahogany fauteuils, 650 iron-framed tip-up seats, a screen, two Ross projectors with BTH motors, a slide projector, two generating sets with 20hp motors, electric fans, a vacuum cleaner, mahogany kiosk and pay desk, etc.

The auditorium re-opened on Friday 31 October 1930 as the Prince's Amusement Hall with an eighteen-hole miniature golf course, rifle shoot, darts games, dancing, a resident pianist, and café. It had two entrances, on Church Path and Tamworth Road, while the elaborate cinema entrance became separate retail premises. In 1931, whist drives were held. By 1941, the place had become Mecca's Palais Dance Hall, entered on Church Path.

The hall was demolished in the 1980s to make way for a small car park and part of an office block. Until then, its entrance doors and old publicity frames for film stills could still be seen. Even in 1989, one side wall survived, attached to adjacent property, and the recess for a publicity frame could be seen on the end. Church Path still exists as a short cut between North End and Tamworth Road.

On North End, the Prince's name remained highly visible, painted on the side walls just below the dome, as late as 1956. The shell-like upper entrance was filled in and the ground floor turned into retail space, used in 2006 by the o2 mobile phone shop. The white-painted dome remains a striking feature in North End.

Picture House/Odeon, No. 108 North End

The rebuilt Picture House was the start of a new wave of cinema construction, the first of the large cinemas that would dominate film exhibition in the Borough. It opened on the Saturday afternoon of 21 April 1928 at 3 p.m. by the Mayoress of Croydon who cut a tape stretched across the stage, whereupon the auditorium darkened, the curtains gently opened, a picture of the King slowly came up on the screen, and those present sang the National Anthem. A little surprisingly, this opening performance (with proceeds to charity) did not attract a full house. The programme, for that one day only, was Richard Dix in *Man Power* and Warner Baxter in *Drums of the Desert*.

The architect of the new Picture House was Mr Clayton of the Brighton practice of Clayton & Black. The design of the auditorium with its straight side walls, curved ceiling, decorated plaster bands and caryatids on the side walls was traditional and unadventurous and must have seemed very old-fashioned within a few years.

The auditorium was twice the height of the old one (the site itself does not seem to have been enlarged), and it seated 1,280 in stalls and balcony with the projection room somewhat unusually placed under the balcony, giving a more direct and comparatively short throw to the screen. This did mean that the upstairs seating was set rather too high for ideal viewing. A Jones tracker action 2-manual straight organ with seventeen speaking stops, originally installed at the Marble Arch Pavilion in 1914, was moved here. There was also a tea lounge.

The balcony was approached by stairs just inside the entrance to the right while the stalls were reached by proceeding past the staircase to the end of a corridor. There was no conventional foyer and the lack of space meant that the main paybox window had to be rather awkwardly situated under the stairs to the circle, so that patrons had to backtrack after obtaining their tickets. There may have been a separate paybox on a landing halfway to the circle, as was certainly established for a while in the 1950s. The last paybox was sited on the ground floor well beyond the stairs.

Electric Theatres (1908) Ltd were still the operators of the Picture House. The company was now headed by Eric Hakim, a prominent figure in the film trade of the 1930s, who brought in an orchestra leader from another of his cinemas – the Academy in Oxford Street – to head the fourteen musicians at Croydon.

Although the Hippodrome had the glory of bringing talking features to the area, to the Picture House belongs the credit for introducing, a month earlier, 'British talking pictures direct from the Tivoli Strand'. These were DeForest Phonofilms, shorts that had first reached the Tivoli in 1925 after playing at the Empire Exhibition at Wembley. They were shown from 7 January 1929 in support of silent features, and during that month included *The Fire Brigade* with Robb Wilton and *The Barrister* with George Robey. However, on 4 February, the Hippodrome opened with *The Singing Fool*, a part-talkie with the much more convincing Vitaphone process. The Picture House fought back with the world premiere of a new British silent feature, *The First Born*, on 22 July but by then sound was all the rage and the Picture House tied in a race with the Davis Theatre to be the second Croydon cinema to introduce it properly. Both installed the Western Electric optical sound system and had it functioning from Monday 5 August 1929. The Picture House announced a huge line-up of fifty talkies. Silent films continued to be shown for some time and the orchestra was retained while these were played off.

In 1936, the Picture House was acquired by the rapidly expanding Odeon circuit and from Friday 11 September it was renamed the Odeon. The organ was removed as being out of date (no new one replaced it, as the instrument was not favoured by the circuit except in seaside and special locations).

By the end of the decade its seating was 1,220 – 744 in the stalls, 476 upstairs. The Odeon circuit was powerful enough to ensure that the Croydon cinema received a steady flow of top attractions. Its capacity was rather low for such a key location but when Odeon took over the Hippodrome in 1942, the same programme was often shown at both cinemas. (The Davis Theatre was also able to screen some big attractions concurrently with the Odeon.) At any rate, the Odeon was for a great many years a very well attended and profitable cinema. (Odeon also built a brand new cinema in South Norwood which usually showed the same new films as the one in Croydon.)

The town centre Odeon entered the CinemaScope era at the same time as the Hippodrome and the South Norwood Odeon when all three cinemas showed *Sign of the Pagan* without stereophonic sound for a six-day run commencing 24 January 1955. The Croydon Odeon's wide proscenium

The former Picture House, North End, as the Odeon in March 1937. A much larger name sign was later mounted across the top of the side wall of the exterior, to be visible from the West Croydon direction. (Photograph by John Maltby.)

Above: The auditorium of the Odeon in March 1937. (Photograph by John Maltby.)

Right: The balcony front is cut back for a projection box to be set underneath it, as can be seen in the poor quality illustration (from 1929). The straight throw was ideal for picture quality.

arch permitted an excellent size of 'Scope picture. This was more than five months after CinemaScope with stereophonic sound had first arrived at the Davis and the Granada Thornton Heath: Improvements were made at the Odeon in the spring of 1956 without closing the theatre. Most attention was paid to the entrance areas. A new canopy with name signs in neon was erected, doors were installed across the entrance for the first time, a false ceiling lowered the height of the entrance hall, and old-fashioned brackets, light fittings and advertising displays were swept away in favour of a more modern decor with wood panelling. The auditorium was redecorated with new screen tabs (curtains) and hanging light fittings. Capacity by now was reduced to 1,115 seats.

Above and left: The entrance to the Odeon before and after modernisation in the mid-1950s. Note the awkward position of the stairs to the balcony. The main box office was located under the stairs but balcony tickets could also be purchased upstairs at busy times during part of the cinema's life.

The entrance to the circle at the Odeon after modernisation in the mid-1950s.

The Odeon celebrated its new look with an extended run of the spectacular *Around the World in 80 Days* at increased prices. Terance Casey played preludes on an electronic Compton Melotone organ – as Tony Moss has noted, 'This was a neat ploy on the part of the circuits which lasted until 1960, to avoid paying entertainments tax by having at least a third of the advertised programme *live*'.

The epic *The Ten Commandments* played for four weeks from 12 October 1958. In December 1961, the Odeon Croydon was in the second wave of eight London cinemas which opened *The Guns of Navarone* for a four-week run before its general release. However, it lost out to the Astoria Purley in some later pre-release runs.

The Odeon was subdivided in 1972 to create smaller cinemas and offer more choice. The last show in the old auditorium featured Bette Davis in *Madame Sin* plus Lee Van Cleef in *Bad Man's River*. This theatre only lent itself to twinning (rather than the more common tripling) and had to be closed for the work to be carried out. The circle was extended forward and a new screen erected while a new projection box was built at the back in place of some of the seating. This became the Odeon 2, seating 430. Downstairs, using the old projection room, Odeon 1 was created – this was the old stalls floor with a new low ceiling supported by two pillars in front of the old circle, extending forward to a new, smaller screen. Seating was for 454. The old screen and proscenium arch disappeared. The cost of the conversion was put at £125,000.

The Odeon re-opened on 11 September with Steve McQueen in *Junior Bonner* in Odeon 1 and Liza Minnelli in *Cabaret* in Odeon 2. The new cinemas were not ideal. The downstairs one had a cramped, claustrophobic atmosphere, especially from seats towards the back, while the upstairs auditorium still had the original cinema's old-fashioned ceiling and awkward access.

Left and above: The Odeon's exterior appearance in its final years, seen here in March 1985, and the entrance area at closing later in the year. (Photographs by Keith Skone (left) and Allen Eyles (above).)

Opposite: The upstairs Odeon 2 on the day after closure when the screen has been ripped. Note the new projection box that was built at the back. (Photographs by Allen Eyles.)

This caryatid and other 1928 decorations survived in the upstairs Odeon 2 until closing. (Photograph by Allen Eyles.)

Croydon's Whitgift shopping centre had been built immediately behind and alongside the Odeon's auditoria. In 1985, the cinema was sold for a high price to enable the shopping centre to expand. Audiences had fallen off in recent years although attendances had bounded back in 1985 with films like *Ghostbusters*. The last day of operation was Thursday 31 October 1985 with *Cocoon* showing upstairs and *Peter Pan* downstairs, the latter attracting 6,000 patrons in a week. Within ten minutes of the final evening showing of *Peter Pan*, the seats were being taken up and by the following morning Odeon 1 had been stripped bare and the projection equipment dismantled in both boxes. Such haste suggested that demolition would be immediate, but in fact the auditorium remained standing for several months afterwards. On the night of Friday 16 May 1986 two piles of rubbish were set on fire and a tenth of the building damaged in the blaze that followed. This seemed to spur some action and the roof had been removed by the end of the month and the walls were coming down. It was indicative of the state of British film exhibition at the time that the proceeds from selling the Odeon were not applied to giving Croydon modern replacement Odeon cinemas elsewhere.

In 2006, the front entrance area is occupied by the Couture menswear shop.

Davis Theatre, No. 73 High Street

It lasted just over thirty years but while it was there, Davis' Theatre (later the Davis Theatre) made Croydon a place of real note on the national entertainment map. The auditorium had the second largest seating capacity in Britain when it opened. There were 3,725 seats according to most sources although a figure as high as 3,900 was also mentioned (perhaps this included standing room). Only Green's Playhouse in Glasgow was larger, seating over 4,300. Two later cinemas – Green's Playhouse in Dundee and the Gaumont State at Kilburn in North London – held more seats than the Davis so it became the fourth biggest cinema in Britain.

The cinema took its name from the Davis family who built it, and it was their tenth venture. They had been pioneers in opening picture palaces in the London area before the Great War, the most famous of their early houses being the Marble Arch Pavilion. After the war Mr and Mrs Israel Davis had opened the Shepherd's Bush Pavilion in 1923, seating 2,776, and had made a success of it despite trade scepticism over its huge size.

Croydon was then the centre for half a million people and lacked a modern cinema. Israel Davis and some close friends acquired the site (which opened out at the back where there was a large orchard) from the Croydon Corporation in January 1927. In May of that year, the existing Davis circuit was incorporated into the new Gaumont-British Picture Corporation and Israel's four sons all took up positions with that concern. It seemed diplomatic to grant G-B's request for a financial interest in the new project. Gaumont gained a twenty per cent stake and its chairman, Lt. Col. A.C. Bromhead, was appointed chairman of the new theatre. His brother, Reginald Bromhead, the managing director of Gaumont, was also given a seat on the board.

The exterior of the Davis Theatre, taken in 1928.

Part of the Davis Theatre's rotunda with its island paybox, taken in 1928.

The auditorium of the Davis Theatre.

Above: In this pre-opening shot of the Davis Theatre balcony, the projection beam can be seen coming from the royal circle while workmen's stepladders are in place in the balcony.

Left and below: The rich side-wall decoration of the Davis Theatre. (Left, from John D. Sharp collection, courtesy of Ashley Hards.)

The new theatre was designed by Robert Cromie, and site excavation began in October 1927. The building work was carried out by Grace and Marsh of Waddon. It was necessary to underpin the adjoining property on three sides for a length of 620ft and to an average depth of 18ft. In all, 28,850 cubic yards of earth were excavated and over 2¼ million bricks, 960 tons of cement, 3,150 yards of ballast and 1,960 yards of sand were used in the construction. The theatre covered an area of 35,000 sq ft and was 76ft high from floor to roof. It took one month to assemble the massive girder, containing 3,500 rivets with a 109 ft span, which supported both the mezzanine and the balcony. 500 tons of steelwork were used in all to support the roof and balconies. The flat concrete roof covered an area of 16,750 sq ft.

The construction of the Davis Theatre took thirteen months. Six weeks were lost to bad weather, but it was completed six weeks ahead of the date contractually specified. Two hundred and ninety men were employed daily without one serious accident, and no night work or weekend work was necessary. The electrical installation was designed and supervised by Basil Davis, one of Israel Davis's sons and the chief engineer of Gaumont-British. The cost of the theatre was approximately £250,000.

Although the Davis Theatre had a far more conspicuous entrance than the cinemas in North End, it was not quite as well sited, being on the southern edge of the commercial heart of Croydon (only the Grand Theatre, of the town centre's entertainment venues, was further out of town in that direction). The frontage was floodlit by sixteen lights at night, eight on the wrought-iron and glass

Above: The projection box of the Davis Theatre can be seen at the back of the lower Royal Circle, providing an almost level throw to the screen.

Right: The organ console and safety curtain with its own built-in screen (John D. Sharp collection, courtesy of Ashley Hards).

canopy and four to either side. There were five sets of entrance doors with French glass engraved in a special design. To the left of the entrance was a bon-bon shop with access to the advance booking office and to the restaurant on the mezzanine floor. Behind the main entrance doors was a vestibule with payboxes on each side. This led to the rotunda hall, over sixty feet in diameter, with a striking mosaic floor and central desk. It was overlooked by the mezzanine where the café and a dance floor were located (the café was not licensed to sell alcohol until April 1949).

The stairs to the mezzanine and to the balcony faced the entrance, while the back of the stalls was reached through a further foyer (this also had a lift for patrons and tea service).

The stalls floor held approximately 2,200 seats. The circle had around 1,500 seats. And there were 225 seats in the Royal Circle at mezzanine level: 201 separate, armchair-style seats, which were the best in the house, and twenty-four conventional tip-up seats in the two back rows to either side of the operating room. This had three film projectors directly facing the screen, plus two spotlights and one lantern-slide projector.

The Davis Theatre was planned to combine films with short live shows but the huge 30ft-deep stage was fully equipped to handle even grand opera, and scenery could be flown using a 60ft-high grid. The orchestral platform (for more than twenty musicians) and organ console platform could be raised or lowered. There were three floors of dressing rooms for up to 110 artists, and a miniature cinema with its own projectors for rehearsal purposes. The Davis Theatre had a 4-manual British-built Compton organ with its thousands of pipes and range of percussion effects located over the proscenium, the sound entering the auditorium through a grille across the entire width of the arch. The console was specially designed by the cinema's architect to harmonise with the design treatment of the auditorium. The late organ expert Tony Moss has noted: 'It was the largest unit organ installed by Compton in a cinema, having 21 units (22 ranks). There was also an upright "phantom" piano in the organ chambers, playable from the console. The organ suffered for its placing over the proscenium, because the sound had to travel from the chambers through a curved duct before reaching the audience through the grille. It was nevertheless a fine instrument'.

The proscenium cove had a phosphorescent glow with its concealed lighting on a silver background that was capable of changing through a complete colour cycle, as was the rim lighting around the silver dome of 50ft diameter in the main ceiling. The colour scheme of the auditorium was greys, subdued blues, violets and jade, with the proscenium pelmet and curtains in soft green silk velour.

Alfred Davis had resigned his job as head film booker with Gaumont and became deputy managing director of the Davis Theatre, taking over responsibility for its opening and subsequent management. (His father, Israel, and his mother retired to Monte Carlo in the 1930s.) One advantage of the Gaumont connection was that the Davis obtained its circuit releases on the best possible terms (while retaining the right to reject any it didn't like). However, Gaumont's two representatives on the board successfully opposed the installation of Western Electric's new Vitaphone sound system for the opening, because Gaumont was developing its own talkie equipment. The apparatus went to the Hippodrome instead. (Quite how long the Gaumont stake and booking facility lasted is not clear.)

The Davis Theatre opened to an invited audience on Tuesday 18 December 1928 with the British premiere of a Hollywood silent film, *The Last Command*, starring Emil Jannings, which had a public run from the following day. Prices ranged from 9d to 5s 9d, this top price being more than twice that charged at any other Croydon cinema in 1930 (except for the New Palladium, almost opposite the Davis, which had a top price of 3s 6d). By 1940 the Davis's cheapest seats were still 9d while the most expensive had been reduced to 3s – which was 8d more than the Odeon.

The first resident organist was Alex Ferguson-Taylor. Its second organist from 1931 to 1932 was Charles Saxby, followed by Lloyd Thomas (1932 to 1934) and then Frank Morgan, who stayed from 1934 to 1945.

The Davis Theatre Symphony Orchestra (conducted by Charles Williams, later of *Dream of Olwyn* fame) accompanied the silent films and also played at intervals. After the huge success of the Hippodrome with talkies, the Davis announced in June 1929 that it was installing Western Electric sound, prompting the Picture House and original Palladium to do likewise. In the race that followed, the Davis made its talkie debut on Monday 5 August, the same day as the Picture House. *Movietone Follies of 1929* was presented on a two-week run. Talking films continued thereafter, with the backlog of silent pictures relegated to supporting features. The Davis had MGM's huge success, *The Broadway Melody,* for another rare two week run from 2 September. In its first year of operation, it claimed 1,183,175 admissions.

On New Year's Eve 1933, 2,000 people attended a night watch service to welcome in the New Year. There were live shows from time to time – a Christmas pantomime, *Babes in the Wood,* from 28 December 1936 for a week (with a lesser Hollywood film, Jane Withers in *Little Miss Nobody*), a 'mammoth' circus along with the film *The Three Maxims* in February 1937. The improved Western Electric Mirrophonic sound system was installed from Monday 11 October 1937. From 26 September 1938, the Davis began an exclusive area run of the Disney sensation, *Snow White and the Seven Dwarfs,* for a week. The late John House recalled: 'I was in the audience watching *Snow White* when the film was stopped, the house lighting came up and the manager appeared on stage to announce that Chamberlain had returned from his meeting with Hitler with the famous agreement. There was tumultuous applause from the audience, convinced that the threat of war had been averted'.

There is some confusion as to whether the all-time record of 54,000 admissions in a week was achieved by *Snow White* (with 11,000 attendances in a single day) or by *Cavalcade,* shown in October 1933. After its first ten years of operation, in December 1938, the Davis declared that it had sold 13½ million tickets (an average of 26,000 admissions a week, helped by Sunday opening from 1932) and shown more than double the quota of British films required by law. The theatre opened at 11.30 a.m. (Sundays from 5 p.m.) and closed at 10 p.m. A sixteen-page publicity brochure, *The Davis Standard,* was issued six times a year until the Second World War. This gave illustrated details of forthcoming attractions.

The Second World War had a serious effect when the London Blitz started in the autumn of 1940. Audience numbers temporarily fell to less than a thousand at weekends and patrons in the balcony moved to the back of the stalls during air-raid warnings for greater protection. But attendances picked up as the cinema provided welcome relief from the stress of the continuing war. However, on Friday 14 January 1944, a single German plane, making a sneak attack that failed to trigger the sirens, dropped a couple of heavy bombs on Croydon. One went through the roof of the Davis and landed in the centre of the stalls. The bomb itself did not explode but split in two as it penetrated the roof and the sheer weight of the missile and the explosion of the detonator killed six and injured twenty-five. There were 2,000 people in the Davis at the time, watching Joan Davis in the supporting film *Two Senoritas.* Had the bomb exploded, it would have killed hundreds. Those who did lose their lives were Mrs Jean Clark, William Hufton, Joan Harbert, and three soldiers: Cpl J. Wilson, Private James Broadgate, and a Canadian, Ernest Otto Meili. The hole in the ceiling, a small hole in the floor and a few wrecked seats were the only tangible evidence afterwards, and repairs enabled the Davis to carry on.

Besides the Gaumont release, the theatre now sometimes showed the same film as the Odeon and so had access to two of the major circuit releases (the third was the ABC programme, played at the Savoy). As surmised in the history of the Odeon (formerly the Picture House), the Davis was probably able to obtain the Odeon programme because the Odeon was on the smallish side and couldn't cope on its own with the demand for really popular attractions. This arrangement continued to operate in the early 1950s when Odeon hits like *The Lavender Hill Mob, The Snows of Kilimanjaro* and *The Caine Mutiny* played at the Davis concurrently (after which the Davis was frozen out by the Hippodrome regularly taking the Odeon release along with the Odeon itself.) The Davis had gained unwelcome competition when it showed the Gaumont release as this could also be played by the Granada Thornton Heath and Astoria Purley.

After the Second World War, the Davis began presenting many live shows, both in place of and additional to the film programmes. Sunday afternoons were a good time because film programmes were only allowed from late afternoon. Sir Thomas Beecham had conducted the London Philharmonic Orchestra there on 29 January 1939 and 8 October 1939. Beecham then conducted the inaugural performance of the Royal Philharmonic Orchestra on 15 September 1946. The singing star Jeanette MacDonald appeared for a sell-out concert on 7 July 1946.

More daring was the booking of some opera, ballet and musical companies for an entire week or longer from September 1946. These live shows risked alienating regular picturegoers but the displaced film programmes were snapped up by the Hippodrome or Palladium. While a stage crew and an advance booking office increased costs, higher prices made a successful live presentation far more profitable than an average film presentation. The Davis ventured into pantomime and ice shows and stage musicals. Productions of *Peter Pan* featured Mary Morris (April 1947) and Margaret Lockwood (April 1950). *Annie Get Your Gun* and *King's Rhapsody* both ran for three weeks (in May 1950 and from Christmas 1951 respectively). However, in 1950/51 the Davis proved too big to support stage stars in straight plays like *Harvey, Pygmalion* and *The Second Mrs Tanqueray* (even with the rear circle and rear stalls roped off).

The Davis sometimes showed an independent streak in its film programming. It would bring back popular films like *The Secret Life of Walter Mitty* and *The African Queen* a few weeks after they had been shown at the Savoy or Odeon rather than take the week's Gaumont release. It occasionally booked a strong independent release like *The Thing from Another World,* an X-certificate thriller, or exploitable 'off-circuit' fare like *Tobor The Great* (with the titular robot parading the streets as a publicity stunt). It revived *King Kong* together with *Bringing Up Baby.* It even played the French X-film *The Seven Deadly Sins.* It would sometimes bolster its main features with stronger supporting films rather than the ones shown elsewhere.

In the early 1950s, the iron and glass canopy above the entrance was replaced and all the floodlights were removed, though four brackets were left to each side. The main neon sign was replaced with neon letters below the cornice rather than on a panel above, and the vertical signs rearranged so that it said DAVIS on the nearest and THEATRE on the furthest whichever direction one approached.

The Davis took a chance on installing a 24ft-wide television screen in collaboration with Croydon Corporation to present the Coronation of Queen Elizabeth II as it happened on 2 June 1953, watched by a full house from 10 a.m. to 5 p.m. The theatre exploited the wave of interest in 3D films with the second feature to open in Britain, after *Bwana Devil*, a minor Hollywood thriller, *The Man in the Dark*, which had a world premiere run from Friday 17 April to 30 April 1953, shown for most of the run four times daily with Reginald Stone at the organ (he did three winter seasons at the Davis from 1952). A 25ft by 20ft 'metallised, sprayed plastic' screen was fitted for 3D and two additional projectors installed so that the film could run without an intermission (two projectors had to show the picture simultaneously). The audience was issued with proper Polaroid glasses to view it. A spy from Granada Theatres reported to head office: 'The screen proved most unsatisfactory; was patchy and leaden, resulting in a persistently cloudy effect and possibly a loss of the illusion in dim shots. The light on the screen was inadequate due to the unavailability of the correct carbon trim ... the picture in my opinion rates mediocre second feature'.

While the Savoy was closed by fire for much of 1953, the Davis helped itself to the best of the ABC releases. It was one of the first places to sign up for CinemaScope with stereophonic sound when 20th Century-Fox guaranteed to supply all its films in the process to independent exhibitors and smaller chains that installed the necessary equipment. A 50ft-wide screen was flown in from the United States and forty-six loudspeakers were installed around the auditorium besides those behind the giant screen. The Davis presented the inaugural CinemaScope film, *The Robe*, for three weeks from Sunday 8 August 1954 (the Granada Thornton Heath showed it concurrently for a week from the following day). The Davis booked *The King and I* from 14 October 1956 on a two-week pre-release run (exclusive to the area), concurrent with London's West End. It still had access to the Gaumont release – and was the only South London cinema that dared show *Rock Around The Clock* on the Sunday when that was being plagued by unruly audiences – twenty youths climbed onto the stage and danced in front of the picture during the last ten minutes and the police had to restore order. Evening shows during the week included an organ interlude; one wonders how the organist went down with the fans of rock 'n' roll.

The Davis interrupted films for one-day twice-nightly live concerts. Besides rock star Bill Haley and his Comets (who played two days: 4 and 5 March 1957), the many musical stars who performed in person in the fifties included Maurice Chevalier (1 February 1953), Frankie Laine (17 October 1954), Gracie Fields (15 December 1954), Liberace (7 October 1956), Paul Anka (22 March 1958) and Mario Lanza (23 March 1958). Jazz concerts and boxing matches also occupied the stage.

This nearly full house dates from around 1950 (CTA/Tony Moss Collection.)

These advertisements show a 3D film, big screen television, the first CinemaScope attraction, and a stage show at the Davis in 1953 and 1954.

The greatest coup among the Davis's live attractions was the booking of the Bolshoi Ballet for whose performances from Wednesday 31 October to Friday 2 November 1956, the only ones given outside Covent Garden, the ticket queue stretched to East Croydon station, much of it waiting all night. The Russians wanted to perform for the British people as well as the Covent Garden elite and the Davis was their choice of venue. Part of the Bolshoi's performances were recorded for the film *The Bolshoi Ballet,* which played a special engagement on the Davis screen from 30 December 1957 in separate performances with Eileen Joyce giving piano recitals and Molly Forbes at the organ (she was resident organist for two years). However, the combination did not attract large audiences.

During the late 1950s, declining cinema attendances, a shortage of new films and reduced access to the more popular ones posed a serious problem for the Davis Theatre's management. The restaurant shut in 1957 (this still had a Compton Melotone organ which both Reginald Stone and Molly Forbes had played as part of their duties). The Gaumont and Fox release streams on which the Davis had relied were about to be closed down with their best pictures going in future to the town's Odeon as part of a new 'Rank Release', leaving the Davis with the leftovers and occasional plums of the 'National Release'. The Odeon and ABC (former Savoy) would share the pick of the new pictures, leaving the Davis Theatre increasingly out in the cold. And staying at home had become more attractive, especially since the arrival of ITV in 1955. The Davis was still huge: undated seating plans, probably from this period, show a seating capacity of 3,657: 2,002 in the stalls; 1,430 in the circle; and 225 in the Royal circle (it is clear from the numbering that two seats had been removed from the centre of each of the five back rows of the circle to create an extra gangway).

The Davis Theatre in April 1959, shortly before closure. (CTA/Tony Moss Collection.)

Plans to close and demolish the Davis were first made public in mid-December 1958, two months after the adverse new release scheme was announced. Alfred Davis was chairman of a development company formed to take over the Davis Theatre and replace it with a multi-storey block of offices and shops. The same company had also acquired the freehold of the Grand Theatre and proposed a similar fate for that, too.

The Grand closed down on 18 April 1959 and was razed, despite a wave of protest at the loss of the town's only live theatre. A petition carried 40,000 signatures. An office block, Grosvenor House, stands on the site.

At this time, plans for the Fairfield Halls had been drawn up and an artist's sketch of the exterior was published in the Croydon press. Croydon Council's Planning and Development Committee turned down an unofficial proposal that the Council should acquire the Davis as an alternative to proceeding with the Fairfield Halls scheme. The committee also declined to buy the Grand and restore it (at an estimated cost of £100,000).

The last live show at the Davis was 'Jazz at the Philharmonic' on Sunday 10 May 1959 with Ella Fitzgerald and the Gene Krupa Quartet. The Davis Theatre closed on Saturday 23 May 1959 after a week's run of *Tom Thumb* (which had been first shown in Croydon at the ABC in January) plus *Andy Hardy Comes Home*. The Davis could have closed with a new release, Hammer Films' version of *The Hound of the Baskervilles,* but preferred to end with a family show for the Whitsun holiday. Before the last audience left, the organist Reginald Hayward (who was also the theatre's last manager) played 'We'll Meet Again' and 'Auld Lang Syne'.

The theatre's contents were auctioned on site on 22, 23 and 24 June. The organ was offered to Croydon Corporation for the Fairfield Halls, where it would have made a truly excellent concert instrument. Instead, some ranks of the organ went to St John's Church, Romford, with the remainder, along with the console, being split up.

An undistinguished office block, Davis House, and car parking space occupy the site of the auditorium while a nondescript row of shops stands on the street frontage. In 2005, the Cinema Theatre Association placed a plaque commemorating the Davis on an adjacent building erected about the same time as the Davis. This organisation also published Alfred Davis's autobiographical notes in its annual magazine *Picture House* (issue No. 30, 2005), plus an article demonstrating the difficulties of programming the Davis Theatre in its last few months.

More than three years after the Davis closed, the Fairfield Halls opened to provide Croydon with a new theatre and concert hall. No one could seriously argue that the complex is any match in design and atmosphere for the Grand and Davis Theatres, buildings that would have been saved if Croydon Council had placed preserving the best of its past above encouraging an early office building boom.

Two surviving buildings, both listed, give an impression of what the Davis auditorium looked like. In January 1929, the Davis family teamed with Gaumont-British to build a Davis Theatre in Hammersmith, again designed by Robert Cromie. In July 1930 Gaumont took over entirely and opened it as the Gaumont Palace cinema, seating 3,560. This is now the Apollo Hammersmith, a live venue. Cromie also designed the Regal (later ABC) cinema at Kingston-on-Thames in a similar style to the Davis. This is currently a bingo hall. Neither is as elaborate or lavish in design as the Davis Theatre.

Empire/Eros, No. 94 North End

The Empire opened in 1906 as a £30,000 reconstruction of the former National Hall/Grand Theatre of Varieties to the design of architect W.G.R. Sprague for Gardiner Hales. It had a long narrow entrance on North End which one ascended to enter the foyer. The auditorium extended to the right, being set at right angles. The outside wall at the rear of the auditorium met the screen end wall of the Picture House/Odeon.

Films were included in the variety bills in the Empire's early years, but it was essentially a music hall until it went over to pictures in November 1930, presumably hoping to fill the gap left by the recent closure of both the Prince's and the Palladium in North End. The opening programme was all-talking: Cliff Edwards in *What Price Melody?* plus Bob Steele in *Near the Rainbow's End* plus Movietone News. Soon, however, live variety acts were added in support of the films.

There were clearly too many picture houses in central Croydon as its operators, Twentieth Century Cinemas (nothing to do with 20th Century-Fox), contracted for Moss Empires to run the Empire as a variety theatre again from 5 September 1938. Films were shown only on Sundays, together with a stage show. Later on, the well-known Hyams brothers presented the live entertainment here and they purchased the building in February 1946. Live shows continued until the week ending 9 May 1953 when Phil Hyams declared that the Empire had lost £11,000 over the past two years and the show *Soldiers in Skirts* became the last live presentation.

The building then underwent a week of modernisation that included a modification of the entrance to give direct access to the stalls through a disused bar. It re-opened as the Eros Cinema, a sister to one at Rushey Green, Catford, in a former live theatre there (the Hyams also ran a distribution company called Eros Films). Programmes concentrated on spicy X certificate Continental double bills (the first was *Wild Boy* plus *Rashomon)* and it advertised as the Eros Continental. On Sundays conventional reissue programmes were shown.

It quickly became very eclectic in its programming. The X films continued but at holiday periods U-certificate shows for the kids were shown, often featuring some of the Hollywood classic features reissued by Eros Films. The Eros jumped on the 3D bandwagon after the Davis and gave first runs to films like *It Came from Outer Space* and *Sangaree,* issuing patrons with dark, plastic-rimmed Polaroid glasses rather than cheap cardboard ones with red and green gelatine. These were loaned free of charge and a special announcement requested the return of these glasses because of their high cost, with staff covering the exits to stop small boys escaping with them. The Eros also showed some of the 20th Century-Fox CinemaScope films that didn't get into the Davis, beginning with *Hell and High Water* on 20 February 1955.

Rumours of impending closure were denied in February 1959. But the Eros was acquired by a Mitcham development company and it closed, only a week after the Davis, on Saturday 30 May 1959. The final programme was a Fox CinemaScope drama *Compulsion* supported by an Eros reissue of an old Paramount western, *Streets of Laredo.*

The building was completely demolished. Although planning permission was obtained in 1961 to replace it with a six-floor office block with three shops and an underground cinema seating 500 plus a car park for fifty vehicles, the old entrance became an entrance to the Whitgift shopping centre while the auditorium area made way for shops.

Above and top right: The Eros at closing in 1959. (Photographs by Michael Thomas.)

Right: The entrance to the Eros. (Courtesy of Richard Norman.)

The exterior and foyer of the Savoy in March 1936. The stalls of the Savoy were reached by descending stairs in the centre of the entrance hall. Staircase to each side took patrons to the balcony with payboxes between. This layout was much favoured by the ABC circuit.

Savoy/ABC/Cannon/Safari, Broad Green, West Croydon

The centrally placed Hippodrome was too small and old-fashioned to remain the local outlet of the rapidly expanding ABC circuit and it looked for space to build a much larger cinema, settling on part of a site at Broad Green created in early 1933 by the demolition of old houses unoccupied since they were used by troops in the First World War. Despite being on the fringe of the town centre, this Croydon cinema became one of the most successful on the circuit. Seating 2,276 (not unusually large for ABC cinemas in more populous areas), it was second in size only to the Davis Theatre in the Borough of Croydon. There was a small free car park to the left.

The Savoy opened at 2 p.m. on Monday 9 March 1936 with the ABC South London release programme of the week. As a matter of policy ABC had unostentatious launches, confident of the quality of their programmes and the comfort of their theatres to attract patrons. The initial programme was *Mary Burns, Fugitive,* starring Sylvia Sidney, supported by *Music Hath Charms* featuring Henry Hall and the BBC Dance Orchestra, Laurel and Hardy in *Thicker Than Water,* and the circuit's own newsreel, the Pathé Super Sound Gazette. The Savoy's manager was E. W. Bassill, who had been the first manager of the Davis Theatre. The Savoy offered all the stalls for 6d and the entire circle for 1s before 3.30 p.m. The rear stalls were charged at 1s after that time, while the circle cost 1s 6d (front) and 1s 3d (rear) rising on Saturdays, Sundays and Bank Holidays to 2s and 1s 6d respectively.

The Savoy was designed in the offices of the circuit's architect, William R. Glen, in very much the characteristic circuit style, except that the auditorium was on the dull and uninteresting side (unlike ABC's splendid Regal at Streatham, for example). The enormous circle seated around 1,100 and the stalls 1,200.

Above and below: The lighting of the Savoy's auditorium in these 1936 photographs is concealed in troughs across the ceiling and on the side walls (a laylight in the ceiling is not switched on). The stencilled designs on the walls and ceiling helped add interest to the rather dull scheme – the plain horizontal bars of the grilles of the ante-proscenium were particularly unimaginative. As in most purpose-built ABC cinemas, exits were provided at the front of the balcony on both sides.

A lofty, spacious, inviting entrance hall had elaborate light fittings overhead. Two payboxes were situated between the sets of stairs. Further inner vestibules served stalls and circle while downstairs there was a considerable standing area to one side for patrons to wait for seats when the house was full. As they already had their tickets, this considerably speeded up filling the house for the next performance.

The seats were upholstered in orange-coloured mohair velvet with sponge rubber armrests covered in green (lesser cinemas had wooden armrests). There was a small orchestra pit (covered in the photograph by artificial flowers) and a stage area to allow theatrical turns to be included in the programme when required.

Although no organ was actually installed, there was an organ well and space for organ chambers to the left of the proscenium. The inner grille would have been the outlet for the chambers. As Tony Moss has observed, it is all the more surprising that no Compton was provided given the popularity of the organ at the Davis. (There were occasions in the 1950s when a Hammond or similar electronic organ was specially brought in for a while, as when Robinson Cleaver played preludes to an extended run of *The Nun's Story* in 1959 as a device to reduce Entertainments Tax by having a substantial part of the show live.)

The Savoy took the usually strong ABC circuit release of the week. Programmes generally ran for six days but *Gone With the Wind* had a two-week run when it played here in September 1942 concurrently with ABC's Regal Purley and Rex Norbury. The film returned in July 1944, and the artist Norman Partridge recalled 'seeing it during a doodlebug alert when the only thing to do was duck under the seat when that terrifying sound in the sky was heard, plainly audible in the cinema above the sound of Clark Gable's voice.'

After the war, a huge triangle sign in red, blue and white neon with the Savoy name inserted in green was mounted on the front of the cinema but it wasn't until the night of Saturday 2 April 1949 that post-war restrictions on power consumption were relaxed and this sign, together with neon displays at Croydon's other cinemas, could be switched on.

The Savoy's career was unexpectedly interrupted when one of the biggest local blazes in years broke out during the early hours of Monday 30 March 1953 after the first day's showings of the Gary Cooper western *Springfield Rifle* supported by *Mantrap*. (The Savoy had become one of the first cinemas to play new films from Sundays instead of a revival programme on that day.) One hundred firemen tackled the flames using three 100ft-high turntable ladders. Although the entrance hall and inner foyers were saved, the auditorium and stage area were gutted. So intense was the fire that every seat was devoured, leaving the standards twisted and partially melted, while much of the plasterwork was reduced to powder, and the glass in the exit signs had dissolved. The cause was believed to have been an electrical fault.

Before the cinema could re-open, much of the steelwork supporting the roof had to be replaced and an entirely new ceiling and proscenium arch constructed. As Tony Moss remembered: 'The new proscenium followed the line of the previous orchestra pit and carried a lovely pair of house tabs in gold with a maroon fringe. They proved to be too heavy for the tab-control mechanism and were removed to the Regal Bexleyheath'. The original wooden stalls floor was replaced by a layer of concrete faced with asphalt and carpeted. The chief architect of ABC at the time, C.J. Foster, was forced to use cheap materials because of post-war government restrictions on how much money could be spent. The walls were resurfaced in asbestos wallboard finished in mushroom pink with gold intersection fillets. Sections of drapes, illuminated from above, helped relieve the effect. The ceiling consisted of a maroon-coloured felt-like material fixed to battens, while similar wool serge material was attached to the rear walls, side walls beneath the circle and front of the circle. The new seats, now totalling 2,230, were covered in wine-coloured

Following the fire in 1953, the front of the canopy directs patrons to the nearest ABC cinema, the Rex Norbury.

The auditorium was gutted and all that is left of the seats are the iron frames.

The new proscenium arch at the Savoy after the fire. (CTA/Tony Moss Collection.)

The balcony of the Savoy after the 1953 fire damage was repaired under cost restrictions. (CTA/Tony Moss Collection.)

moquette. Only one coat of paint was permitted to redecorate the foyers and entrance hall. A new screen suitable for 3D films and wide screen was installed. The Savoy's doors re-opened on 27 December with the Esther Williams musical *Dangerous When Wet*.

The cinema was soon showing 3D films like *Phantom of the Rue Morgue*, charging 6d for Polaroid viewers (although the Regal Purley showed the film 'flat'). CinemaScope was introduced (concurrently with the Rex Norbury, another ABC hall) for *The Command*, a western shown for seven days from Sunday 26 September 1954.

On 5 July 1958 the Savoy closed to enable a proper reconstruction of the auditorium to take place. The cinema re-opened on 19 October 1958 with *Ice Cold in Alex* and the new name of

Right and below: The ABC Croydon after the conversion to three screens, taking over five months. The old payboxes now serve the upstairs Screen 1. (These and succeeding ABC triple photographs courtesy of Richard Brazier.)

ABC. Four lozenge-shaped light boxes, mounted vertically on one side of the frontage, carried the three letters of the name, raised in black on a white background, plus a representation of the old triangle logo. The auditorium now seated 2,118 and had been given lavish, modern styling inside. There were both screen and main tabs. The auditorium had never looked better. Unfortunately, no photographs of its new appearance seem to exist.

With the demise of the Davis, the ABC started putting on numerous live shows featuring such stars as Cliff Richard, Billy Fury (he played here three times), the Beatles (Thursday 21 March 1963, when they were fourth on the bill), Gene Pitney, the Everly Brothers, and many more. Bingo was briefly tried out on Sunday afternoons.

By the 1970s the ABC was clearly too large for current requirements and it closed on 20 May 1972 for tripling following the run of an epic called *Waterloo*. The rear circle section behind the crossover became the 650-seat ABC 1 with a new screen and curtains placed in front. The entry stairs in the middle of the crossover of the original circle were still in use, but now brought patrons up in front of the screen. ABC 2 (seating 390) was created on the right hand side of the former stalls area. ABC 3 (seating 187) was created on the left hand side. A large area to the right of ABC 2, the former waiting area for patrons when stalls seating was full, became a licensed bar.

The conversion cost £178,000 and the ABC re-opened on 2 November 1972 with *The Godfather* upstairs (tickets costing 55p and 75p), *Deliverance* in ABC 2 and *The Garden of the Finzi-Continis* in ABC 3 (both charging 55p for all seats).

The ceiling of ABC 1 was painted pink, the walls and side soffits in regal red, nightshade and rose grey, and the carpet was red with the seats in amethyst violet. With its stepped seating affording a clear view of the screen, and with its lush wine-red curtains and concealed lighting at the sides and rear, this became a superior venue for enjoying a film.

ABC 2 was painted in shades of marigold and light stone with the seats covered in turquoise and the screen curtains in orange. ABC 3 had walls and ceiling in a Tuscan shade blending with lemon-coloured seats and screen curtains. By now the ABC circuit was owned by EMI and the lower lozenge-shaped sign on the front carried the EMI logo in place of the triangle.

The most profitable film to play the new three-screen complex was the original *Jaws* which stayed for twenty-six weeks on one or other of the screens and was re-run later as well.

The Cannon Group acquired the ABC circuit in 1986. The cinema was renamed with a new vertical Cannon sign which went up over the weekend of 18/19 October 1986. As the only surviving cinema in the town of Croydon, the Cannon had an unrestricted choice of new films and was well attended.

Ownership passed to Virgin when it took over the entire Cannon-MGM circuit. When Virgin sold most of the traditional cinemas to a new ABC Cinemas company and kept the multiplexes, it sold this one building on Friday 6 December 1996 to an Indian operator who renamed it the Safari after another cinema in Harrow and one in Nairobi. As the Safari, it combined Hindi films with new mainstream releases, usually opening around 5 p.m. but with late night shows, at one time dropping prices to just £2 on Wednesdays.

The arrival of the Warner Cinemas multiplex on Purley Way spelt trouble, as did the overall decline of this part of Croydon with the loss of the old Co-op department store. It attempted a cut-price policy and later closed for a while, but was still showing Hindi films to some indeterminate date in 2003, shortly after the second Warner multiplex arrived in the centre of Croydon and programmed Hindi films on some screens. Plans have been developed to demolish the building and replace it with flats – but in early 2006 it stands, with Safari vertical name sign intact, a once proud and much loved building that has degenerated into an eyesore.

A new paybox at the foot of the stairs to the old stalls served patrons for ABC 2 and 3.

An old waiting area became a bar on the right-hand side of the old stalls area, adjacent to ABC 2.

Above and below: The new Screens 2 (above) and 3 at the ABC Croydon in 1972.

Above and below: Screen 1, the largest auditorium at the tripled ABC Croydon, extending the old balcony.

The Focus cinemas on the site of the Hippodrome on Crown Hill with an old Classic sign remaining high up on the side wall. (Photograph by Keith Skone.)

Classic/Oscar/Focus, Crown Hill

The Classic circuit rather surprisingly opened three new cinemas here on Saturday 26 August 1972, converted from the building, on the site of the former Hippodrome, which had been in retail use as part of British Home Stores. The cinemas were reached up a wide, steep flight of stairs and shared the building with a sauna and discotheque. The auditoria were poorly raked with low ceilings and drapes covering side walls of breeze blocks; some of the projection was by mirrors rather than direct. They were, in design terms, nothing to get excited about, but they were nevertheless a bold undertaking in that they relied on second-run programming for two of the auditoria (with occasional new films not wanted by the ABC or Odeon) and in that the third operated as a cartoon cinema, opening from 11 a.m. to tempt shoppers in the outdoor market to come inside for a relaxing hour or so (the other two screens functioned from 1 p.m. or later).

Classic 1 seated 213 and started off with an eight-day run of *Mutiny on the Buses* plus *The Man Who Haunted Himself.* Classic 2 seated 193 and commenced with *What's Up, Doc?* plus *Ski Raiders* for eight days. The cartoon cinema seated 112 and offered 90-minute programmes of cartoons and short comedies – its prices were 15p for adults, 10p for children and senior citizens. Prices for the feature programmes in Classic 1 and 2 were 50p for adults, 25p for children, and 10p for senior citizens. The cartoon policy was short-lived and double bills of feature films took over here as well. The cinemas passed to the Brent Walker Group from 20 January 1974 and were renamed Oscar 1, 2 and 3. After objections from the Los Angeles Academy of Motion Picture Arts and Sciences over the use of 'Oscar' by Brent Walker's chain of cinemas, the name Focus was substituted from 11 April 1974.

For several years, the cinemas seemed well attended, helped by their central location and value-for-money programming. But they closed after the last performance on Saturday 14 August 1982, part of Brent Walker's withdrawal from film exhibition during that year. The building is occupied in 2006 by a Walkabout pub, a nightclub called Fyeo, and the Loop Poolbar.

Fairfield Halls, Park Lane, Croydon

Croydon Council decided to erect the Fairfield Halls in July 1955 on part of a site where an annual fair was held for centuries until 1866, gaining a reputation for rowdy behaviour by visitors from out of town. Taken over in 1866 by the Brighton Railway Co., the site was in use as a sidings and workshop for the Southern Railway in 1933. The following year, Croydon Corporation bought it to stifle plans for a greyhound racing track.

The complex was built at a cost of £1.25 million and opened by Queen Elizabeth the Queen Mother on 2 November 1962. Its main units are the Concert Hall, the Ashcroft Theatre, and the Arnhem Gallery. Following a show of work by local artist Norman H. Partridge in December 1970, the Fairfield management committee bought eight of his paintings, including some excellent representations of old Croydon cinemas and theatres that have been on display ever since – in 2005 in the entrance corridor at the Ashcroft balcony level.

From the first, the Concert Hall was equipped for cinematographic use, with a huge screen being unrolled and suspended over the orchestral platform. Though subsidiary to live shows, its role as a cinema increased in later years with the decline in the number of Croydon cinemas, enabling it to bring back recent hits and show films of more specialised appeal for the first time in the Croydon area. These were presented at least one day per week, often on several days during school holidays, but generally filling the slacker evenings early in the week. In addition, a number of evenings of archive film were arranged and presented by the late John Huntley. The projection equipment was upgraded in 1986 following the closure of the Odeon. Though not a true cinema in appearance, its 1,552 seats in stepped rows provided an excellent, unimpeded view of the screen.

The Ashcroft Theatre was also equipped to show films and still does so on occasion.

The Concert Hall at the Fairfield Halls, set up for a film show. (Tony Moss Collection/photograph by the late John D. Sharp.)

The David Lean Cinema, which is entered from the right hand side. A wall speaker is visible at top left. (Photograph courtesy of Victoria Pitt.)

David Lean Cinema, Clocktower, Katharine Street

The film director David Lean was born at No. 38 Blenheim Crescent, South Croydon, and his recollections of visiting the Scala have been quoted earlier. Lean died in 1991 and his name was attached to this conversion of the old local studies library into a versatile 68-seat cinema, opened on Friday 3 March 1995 with Peter Jackson's *Heavenly Creatures* and a short film *Home You Go*. It was part of the new £30 million Clocktower complex which included a modern library, exhibitions gallery, tourist information centre, local history museum, café and shop. The David Lean Cinema was equipped to show 35mm and 16mm film and video. A Dolby surround stereo system was installed. The auditorium could also be used for conferences, lectures, presentations and product launches. Although perfectly comfortable, it resembles a smaller screen at a multiplex and its value lies in showing specialised new films and classics that are not to be found in the town's two multiplexes. The cinema, along with the rest of the complex, is closed on Sundays.

Above left and right: In June 2002, Croydon's city centre multiplex looms over Surrey Street with the Grants name (no apostrophe) just visible at the very top. The curved glazing of the central section indicates the colossal height of the foyer. The Warner Village signs have since been replaced with Vue signs. (Photographs by Allen Eyles.)

Warner Village/Vue, Grants, No. 14 High Street

In the 1990s, the town centre was largely dead after 6 p.m. when all the shops closed. There was considerable interest from developers in opening a multiplex cinema as the 'anchor tenant' of larger shopping and leisure developments. Two sites were identified. Six acres of land on the west side of East Croydon station, vacant for thirty years, were the subject of a planning application in April 1997 for a 24-screen cinema, real snow ski slope, children's toboggan run, arena, etc., but the Council was more enthusiastic about the scheme proposed for the former Grant's department store, disused for more than ten years, which would retain the historic Victorian façade on the High Street. Here the developers had a longstanding agreement with Warner Bros to operate a 12- or 14-screen cinema in addition to the company's multiplex on Purley Way. At that time the cinema was likely to be situated over a 500-space car park on the other side of Surrey Street, connected by a bridge to the actual Grant's site. The Grant's scheme went ahead, extending over and largely obliterating Middle Street as new building reached the east side of Surrey Street but did not cross it.

The Warner Village at Grant's Centre (now known as Grants without the apostrophe) opened to the public on Friday 3 May 2002 with ten screens which were located on top of the site with a huge vertical window at the rear on Surrey Street. The multiplex has minimal presence on the

Above left: The free-standing lift tower rising up the foyer of the Warner Village multiplex had been decorated to show Warner Bros. cartoon characters Bugs Bunny and Daffy Duck at work on the side of a skyscraper based on New York City's Chrysler building. In 2006, the lift has been painted a plain red colour following the Vue takeover and the suspended screen has now gone.

Above right: the vast space in front of the refreshment counter was backed by a panoramic painting based on the Warner Bros. classic *Casablanca*. There was a surprising absence of seats in this area. The painting has now been replaced with one promoting Vue Cinemas and Bugs Bunny has gone. Some DVD monitors remain. The tall windows overlooking Surrey Street are to the right. (Photographs by Allen Eyles.)

High Street – its entrance is just a narrow passage with a small name sign overhead. Only by going to the rear of the building does the enormous amount of space taken up by the cinemas become apparent.

The entrance passage opens out at the back into the base of a vast foyer, the height of the tall window with Surrey Street visible below (there is an entrance to a fitness centre below, at ground floor level). An escalator takes cinemagoers to the box office at the next level. From here, another escalator conveys customers to the vast main foyer with a refreshments counter at the back, a games room to one side, and a corridor leading to screens 1, 2 and 3. It takes two further escalators to reach the upper foyer and the entrances to screens 4 to 10. A lift serves all levels but patrons of the upper cinemas have to leave via a staircase to reach the down escalators at the level of the screens below. As at Purley Way, the foyers, press advertising and screen titles all made extensive use of Warner Bros cartoon characters like Bugs Bunny and Daffy Duck – felt by some observers to put off adult cinemagoers.

All ten cinemas at Grants have Dolby surround sound and stadium seating. They are lofty and spacious with huge uncurtained screens and tip-up seating in stadium style (plus rows of flat seating at the front of the larger auditoria). Decoration is minimal but the side walls of the larger screens have uplighters illuminating a vertical yellow band with a protruding semi-circular cap. Principal colours are blue and maroon. The largest cinema (No. 6) seats 398 and the smallest (No. 5) only 88. In between, there were: 171 seats in 1; 194 in 2; 178 in 3; 106 in 4; 170 in 7; 131 in 8; 167 in 9; and 224 in 10. This gave a total of 1,827 compared to 2,064 on two fewer screens at the multiplex on Purley Way.

The multiplex opened on Friday 3 May 2002 as the Warner Village, reflecting Warner Bros' partnership with Australia's Village Roadshow. There was a choice of twelve films in the first week. These included: *Panic Room* (on two screens), *About A Boy, Road Kill, Bend It Like Beckham, The Scorpion King, Show Time* and a Bollywood film *Haan Maine Bhi Pyaar Kiya* as the main attractions, the others having limited showings. The first blockbuster was *Star Wars: Episode II – Attack of the Clones* from 16 May.

The Warner Village circuit was acquired by a company called Vue in March 2003 and the two Croydon cinemas eventually took the Vue name, the Grants site coming first from Friday 9 April 2004.

two

Norbury

Palais de Luxe/Norbury Cinema/Searchlight, (Nos 8/9 King Edward Parade), 1355 London Road

The Palais de Luxe opened on 21 March 1910. It was an adaptation of a 700-seat public hall, the King Edward Hall, the centrepiece of a new parade of shops and flats on Norbury's main road completed in 1906. The entrance to the hall was marked by a canopy with a pitched glass roof that stretched out to the kerb where it was supported on columns. The builder and promoter, Charles Spencer, initially had plans approved in August 1904 for a small cinema to occupy 1355/7 London Road but replaced this with plans, approved in December 1904, for the much larger public hall which stretched further back. This staged Saturday night music concerts in its early years before being used for music hall with films as part of the bill. As a cinema it had a long, narrow shape (74ft by 37ft), 398 seats (including 75 in a balcony), four exits, and a slate roof. The words LIVING PICTURES now appeared horizontally on the sides of the glass canopy. Programmes were shown initially from 3 p.m. to 10.30 p.m. with special children's matinées. There was a threat of competition in March 1911 when plans for a cinema designed by Horace M. Wakley [Wakeley?] for Picture Playhouse Norbury Ltd are mentioned in the trade paper *The Bioscope*.

Patrons in 1914 were noted as particularly liking films based on Shakespeare and novels. Changes of proprietorship seem to have been frequent. In 1920, the Palais de Luxe was renamed the Norbury Cinema. In 1924 it was modernised as part of a £9,000 scheme (architect: Frank Jennings) which added a low, L-shaped dance hall, situated beyond the screen end of the cinema and extending around the front left of the auditorium.

1910 newspaper advertisement (courtesy of Spencer Hobbs).

Norbury's first cinema. The words LIVING PICTURES appear on the side of the glass canopy where earlier the words PUBLIC HALL had been evident. The elaborate decoration of the frontage survived until paint warehouse days – in 2006, it has become windowless and very plain.

In November 1928, the cinema came under the control of H. Guyster, who operated the Stockwell Palladium and Brixton Hill New Royalty. He put in a full stage and created a larger vestibule with six entrance doors.

In the early 1930s the cinema fell on hard times and closed for a year. It re-opened on Easter Monday 2 April 1934 with 859 new seats in place, boasting, 'A Marvellous Transformation Absolutely New Throughout'. The improvements were only marvellous enough to keep it open for a few months.

It returned on Monday 4 February 1935 under new management with a new name, the Searchlight, and a policy of 'cine variety', the films being supported by the Searchlight Orchestra and live entertainers, beginning with Sidney Arnold, 'of C.B. Cochran revue and BBC comedy fame'. The policy failed and the cinema was in the hands of a receiver by May 1935. An unknown offence had resulted in a ban on Sunday opening which was only lifted when new lessees arrived in October 1935 and undertook to give no further cause for complaint. It was again called the Norbury Cinema.

All these difficulties preceded the worst blow of all – the opening, virtually opposite, of the new ABC circuit house, the Rex, with top-flight new films rather than the old ones it played. ABC sought a licence in early October 1936, after construction had begun. Consolidated Cinemas Ltd, current owners of the Norbury Cinema, contested the application on the grounds of 'redundancy', stating that there was hardly sufficient demand for their cinema, let alone two, and that ABC were out to crush the independent operator. But the Council had already rejected 'redundancy' (or 'surfeit') as a reason for turning down new cinema schemes at a meeting in October 1935 and felt that it should not stand in the way of progress and modern buildings.

The Norbury Cinema co-existed with the Rex for a few months before closing in 1937. The glass canopy was taken down for safety reasons when war broke out, and the premises served as a British Restaurant selling cheap meals at 6d. The complex later became a warehouse for Ronson's and Norland paints. It was gutted in the late 1960s to become a supermarket which was part of the Gateway chain in 1989. In 2006, it is the premises of Dreamland Beds with no indication of its long-ago cinema usage.

The Rex Norbury, seen here in June 1946, originally displayed a very small ABC triangle on the brickwork high above its name rather than the two seen here lower down. By the 1950s, these and the original name sign had been replaced by one of the circuit's large triangular signs in red and blue, with the letters of ABC and the name in green below it (like the Regal Purley in the photograph on page 83). The road down the side of the cinema led to a small car park behind.

Rex, London Road

It was Fred Harrington, the father of a local architect, Douglas Harrington, who interested the ABC circuit in taking over this scheme designed by his son.

The Rex opened on a Monday, 4 January 1937, at 2 p.m. (like the Savoy Croydon ten months previously). It was the first of nineteen new outlets opened by the ABC circuit in 1937. The first week's attraction was the Astaire-Rogers musical *Swing Time* supported by Jack Haley in *Mr Cinderella*. Prices of admission were 6d and 1s for the stalls, and 1s 6d and 2s for the circle. Before 3.30 p.m. (3 p.m. Saturdays), all stalls seats were 6d and all circle seats 1s.

The Rex had a pleasant but unremarkable exterior with a lock-up shop on each corner. It was set back from the main road, with its own road for vehicles to drop off patrons. There was a small car park at the rear. The foyer was shallow but wide with stairs to the circle in the centre, doors to the stalls on the far sides, and a paybox and a confectionery counter set into the walls between.

The auditorium was strikingly modern and made a very agreeable setting for an evening's entertainment. It seated 960 in the stalls and 544 in the circle – a total of 1,504. (Trade yearbooks give later seating figures of 1,508 for 1940 and 1,498 in the 1950s.)

Above and below: The auditorium of the Rex Norbury at opening in 1937.

Another view of the auditorium of the Rex Norbury in 1937. Unusually, the only exits from the balcony seem to have been off the centre crossover.

The lighting scheme for the auditorium was very simple and effective. The ceiling seemed to float thanks to concealed lighting along the rim. There was further concealed lighting in domes in the ceiling and under the circle, as well as behind the extension of the circle front onto the side walls. The ventilation grilles were left as plain circular holes in a honeycomb effect that appeared later that same year at the Gaumont Watford and Odeon South Norwood (as well as later at the Odeon Camberwell). The slightly bare effect was relieved by the red and silvery-grey seating, the leaf-patterned carpet, and the stage curtains embroidered with butterflies.

One non-cinematic event that attracted a full house took place in November 1937 when every seat was taken for a peace meeting addressed by George Lansbury. For the hundreds unable to get inside, a second meeting took place in the Rex's car park.

Once ABC had opened its new Regal in Streatham in November 1938, the Rex was hardly necessary to the circuit as Norbury cinemagoers could quite easily reach the Regal, or the Savoy Croydon or the Majestic at Mitcham, which all played the same weekly circuit release as the Rex.

The Rex was profitable enough during the boom years of filmgoing, and benefited while the Savoy Croydon was temporarily closed by fire in 1953. In the 1950s it would occasionally duck a particularly poor release programme to go 'off-circuit', usually playing French films, often an 'exclusive South London presentation' (for example, *Femmes de Paris* in May 1958). It also held the district office for the South London area of the ABC circuit. The nearest opposition was the Granada Thornton Heath, on the same road about a mile away, which played different films but was programmed far more flexibly.

The Rex's future became in doubt when an application was submitted in July 1957 to replace it with a garage. A company spokesman said that it had been losing money recently. Plans for a petrol station were put forward in February 1958, then withdrawn. Occasionally, powerful attractions like *Dunkirk* would still produce full houses and queues outside. Afternoon shows were eliminated on Thursdays and Fridays, then on Mondays and Tuesdays as well, except for school holidays.

The Rex finally closed on Saturday 17 February 1962 after a week's run of the musical *Fanny*. ABC then turned it into the Alpha Bingo Club on Wednesdays, Fridays, Saturdays and Sundays, beginning the following Wednesday, 21 February, when Arthur Haynes made a personal appearance. Norbury at that time was too sophisticated an area to support bingo and the building eventually made way for the Radnor House office block which in 2005 was being converted into 113 flats with a completion date of April 2006.

three

Purley
and
Coulsdon

Palladium/Cinema/Bijou, No. 3 Malcolm Road, Coulsdon

This small purpose-built cinema was erected at a cost of around £860 and seems to have been originally owned by Mrs Laura Ross of Purley. It opened as the Palladium on Easter Monday 1914, originally seating 318 people. The Palladium was then rented by a company newly registered on 22 December 1914, Coulsdon Cinema Ltd, but closed just weeks later on 26 February 1915. Did this company rename it the Cinema? It returned with a succession of owners (Mrs S.A. Smith, Miss E. Hamilton, the South London Cinema Co.) before closing again in 1922, when it may have been known as the Bohemia. It re-opened in 1923 and boasted the word CINEMA on its roof.

In the *Croydon Advertiser* of 19 March 1971, Coulsdon resident Arthur Carter recalled: 'There were two houses a night, with a cut-price matinee on Saturday afternoons. Seeing that the place was run on part-time and unskilled labour, the film was certain to break at least once during a show, and some unfortunate juvenile would be ejected for cheering the hero or booing the villain'.

It had at least three more proprietors (J.W. Thould, Reeve Hides, C.R. Hicks) before closing permanently around 1932. Seating was down to 230 at the beginning of 1929, with a box at the rear for seven people. It became the Bijou for a while in its final years and may have also been known as the Plaza. It was probably forced to close by the competition from the larger, more modern Capitol (later Florida) at nearby Caterham, and it may well not have been suited to showing sound films. Its location, a little way up a side road off the main Brighton Road, was no help either.

The building was taken over by Murray & Sons in 1933/34. In the early 1970s it was a United Dairies depot. In 1987, it had become part of the premises of Maxon Tiling, suppliers of ceramic tiles, and in 2006 it is the Tile Base for wall and floor tiles. The curved top over the entrance may date from later cinema days but the auditorium behind has been extensively or completely rebuilt. See back cover for an exterior photograph in cinema days, from John Gent's collection.

Regal, Nos 92-98 Brighton Road, Purley

Purley had no cinemas at all until 1934 when a race started which was won by the Regal. Before that, a proposal for a cinema to be called the Orpheum had come from a company called Westminster Cinemas which had architect Robert Cromie draw up plans, submitted in January 1931, for a 1,706-seat cinema with overhanging balcony. This was quickly superseded by plans for a 1,570-seat stadium-style building. Tony Moss identified the site as being at the corner of Brighton Road and Old Lodge Lane, opposite the fire station and just beyond the spot where the Regal was built. It was said that the Orpheum would open in October 1931.

The Regal was a private venture by a company chaired by Colonel J. Baldwin Webb with Joseph Cohen as the managing director. The architect was Harold Scott of Birmingham, who was also a director (Scott designed many cinemas, including the Mayfair, later ABC, Tooting). The site on the Brighton Road was well outside the centre of Purley and part of a leisure nucleus that included the Imperial Rink (a bowling alley in 2006).

A largish suburban cinema, the Regal seated 1,106 in the stalls and 472 in the circle, a total of 1,578. The very first film shown, on Monday 26 February 1934, was the appropriately titled Mickey Mouse cartoon, *Building a Building,* which preceded the features *I Live With You* and *Her First Mate.* The programme ran three days, being changed on Thursday. There was the usual café which was still open in the late 1940s.

The Regal Purley just before opening in 1934.

Just a few months later, from 11 June 1934, the Regal was leased by the rapidly growing ABC circuit. By early July it was running ABC's new circuit releases for six days, concurrently with the Hippodrome Croydon, with ABC's Pathetone replacing the Gaumont Graphic newsreel. The Regal's access to a steady stream of generally popular ABC programmes ensured its survival for forty years. Occasionally it would go 'off circuit'. C.J. Bird, who worked there from 1964, has observed: 'The cinema had a certain smell, which I never found in other [ABC cinemas]. I think it was the fabrics and, after time off, it would welcome me back as I walked in the doors. The staff were, in the main, middle-aged and a nice type who enjoyed coming to work for a rather meagre wage. The patrons were mainly upper middle class and, except on Sunday first house, did not cause trouble. We did not always play the ABC circuit programme, finding that "Purley people" would not come to horror programmes (Hammer type) and did not enjoy American sex films but would come to English or French sex films. We would therefore go 'off-circuit' when these types of programmes were booked and play re-releases'. Local patron Bryan Prosper noted in a letter written in 2000: 'There was always a draught in the circle, no matter where one sat. In winter or summer – always a draught!'

Unlike most of the other ABC cinemas that survived into the 1960s, the Regal's name was never changed to ABC, and it retained the triangular sign in red, blue, green and white neon that identified the circuit from the 1950s.

In June 1969, ABC purchased the freehold of the cinema and the shops incorporated in its frontage for a price of around £100,000. EMI acquired the S&K chain in 1967, including the

The auditorium of the Regal Purley in 1934. Note the sunburst effect from ribs on the ceiling but with concealed lighting further back. The decorative panel shows a silhouetted female in the forest setting.

rival Astoria Purley, and then the ABC circuit in February 1969, thereby taking over both the local cinemas. EMI decided to convert one to multi-screen operation and close the other. The Regal was shut after a week's run of *Don't Look Now* with *The Wicker Man,* which ended on Saturday 16 February 1974. The building was then leased by the Star group for bingo and later became the Lesleen Bingo and Social Club in other hands. Only the stalls floor was used. A false ceiling was later suspended over the front stalls, obscuring most of the decorative detail and leaving the balcony disused. Externally, the Regal name remained on a large vertical sign dating from the 1960s (lettering in white on a blue background). Original monograms of the 'R' in Regal were also visible in the leaded glass. A dance school, entered from the side, occupied the former café space above the entrance.

After the Cannon Group bought EMI's cinemas in 1986, this was one of thirty properties put up for auction as an investment on 5 March 1987 when it was stated to be producing an income of £21,800 per annum with reviews from 1988. It was sold for £270,000. Bingo finished on 31 August 1996 and the building was demolished the following autumn. It has been replaced by the dreary three-storey Regal House (the name is on a small sign on a side wall) which has two retail units on the main road – Hein Gericko and American Golf – with six flats, accessed at the rear, above them.

In this July 1964 view, the original Regal sign has been supplemented by two others in different styles! Only the vertical sign at right survived into its bingo days and demolition.

Astoria/Cannon/MGM/ABC, High Street, Purley

This Purley building overcame a troublesome start to become one of the borough's longest running cinemas. It was conceived as the latest of a small chain of Astorias started at Brighton and headed by veteran exhibitor E.E. Lyons. Astoria (Purley) Ltd was formed in May 1933 and architect F.C. Mitchell's plans for the site in the centre of Purley were submitted in October 1933. The company experienced considerable difficulty in raising sufficient capital and the builders, T.J. Braybon & Son of Brighton, eventually agreed to advance £16,000. It had originally been intended to open the Astoria in December 1933 and there was considerable panic when construction started on the Regal cinema out on London Road. The Astoria was hurriedly erected in the short time of twenty weeks with the builders working night and day and finishing nine days ahead of schedule. Even so, it opened several weeks after the Regal. The cost of the Astoria was around £50,000.

Seating 1,550, the Astoria had a 12ft-deep stage and was equipped for live shows with three dressing rooms. Its 3-manual Compton organ had five ranks and a console (one of the cheaper wooden-block tower surrounds with an ornate music-stand) which rose on a lift. There was the usual café or tea lounge outside the balcony entrance. The auditorium was mainly lit from a dome in the ceiling, concealed lighting from the caps of pilasters on the side walls, and from coves around the 34ft-wide proscenium arch. There was a free car park.

Exterior of the Astoria Purley in 1934. Strips of vertical neon reinforce the tall windows and slightly protruding edge of the centre section above canopy level. The buildings to the right survive in 2006. A set of photographs preserved by the Astoria's builders, T.J. Braybon & Son, presented to John Fernee and passed on to the author of this book, enables a thorough look at this cinema in 1934.

The Astoria Purley – foyer with paybox.

The Astoria styled itself The Cinema Supreme. The opening attraction on Easter Monday 2 April 1934 was *The Way to Love* with Maurice Chevalier plus *Ever in My Heart* with Barbara Stanwyck, a Laurel and Hardy short and Robin Richmond on the mighty Compton. (Richmond was the first resident organist. He was succeeded by Andrew Fenner in 1934/5 and Peter Kenyon in 1935/7. After this, the organ was apparently little used, though it was well looked after and fully playable in the early 1950s.)

In its early days, the Astoria had to show films after they had been seen not only in central Croydon but also in Caterham. Although it had the advantage of a central location, it lacked the booking strength that the Regal obtained when it became part of the ABC circuit and the town wasn't big enough to support two expensive new cinemas with 3,128 seats between them. The Astoria's problems were aggravated by the death of E.E. Lyons on 9 August 1934 and by the fine summer of that year which kept people from the pictures. Takings at the Astoria averaged £250 a week, half the anticipated figure. By December, some new films were playing simultaneously with the Picture House Croydon.

Desperate attempts were made to sell the cinema but it was not an attractive proposition and Astoria (Purley) Ltd went into compulsory liquidation in June 1935. The cinema then gained a new proprietor, H.J. Morgenstern (H.J.M. Cinemas) and continued to show some new releases

Above and opposite above: The Astoria Purley in 1934 – balcony lounge with entrance at right to the 'Dress Circle' and the café area.

concurrently with the Picture House (later Odeon) Croydon. At the end of February 1949 it was taken over by the sizeable Shipman & King circuit which was able to obtain the week's Odeon or Gaumont circuit booking in tandem with central Croydon. The new era of CinemaScope arrived here on 22 November 1954 with a Gaumont circuit release, *The Black Shield of Falworth*, shown concurrently with the Davis Theatre and the Granada at Thornton Heath.

Richard Gray recalled the Astoria:

It was quite plain inside really and the best thing was the illuminated proscenium arch which always had several colours working, usually changing to a blue/white light just before the tabs parted, with the censor's certificate played on them closed. The circle entrance had a neat sign over its door marked 'Dress Circle' – so appropriate for Purley in 1934. The café had gone by the mid-1960s but I recall a few chairs dotted about outside the circle entrance. My mother always referred to it as the 'little' Astoria (with 1,500 seats!) – possibly, in contrast to the Davis where one could often see the same offering, it was. I remember S&K's trailer leaders were very distinctive and tastefully discreet – serifed lettering against a kind of muted wickerwork background. I never saw the organ played, just a shrouded lump in front of the stage.

Right: The Astoria Purley in 1934 – the Ladies'
room, its curtained entrance seen in the
photograph of the balcony lounge on the facing
page.

Above and left: The auditorium of the Astoria Purley in 1934. Note the concealed lighting of the proscenium arch and the illuminated heads of the pilasters on the side wall, plus the organ console in raised position.

The auditorium of the Astoria
Purley in 1934.

In 1964, the Astoria was the one Shipman & King cinema included in the Premiere Showcase
line-up of eight London suburban cinemas that screened the James Bond smash hit *Goldfinger*
concurrently with the West End at increased prices. The nearest competition was the Odeon
Streatham. It had similar pre-release bookings later on. The Astoria was not as significant as the
other cinemas in these groupings but S&K's inclusion gained its co-operation in this break with
the normal release pattern.

The Astoria drew adverse publicity in the local press when it revived *Snow White and the Seven
Dwarfs* one winter. People were queuing outside and one lady, who was allowed to visit the toilet
upstairs, slipped into the circle and found many vacant seats, reporting this back to the others
waiting outside. In a 1990 letter, Bryan Prosper recalls that the seating layout of the stalls later
differed from that depicted in the 1934 photograph to the rear of the auditorium: 'The centre
gangway changed direction half way, meeting up with the cross gangway. If you went in walking
down the centre during a performance, the chances were you would find yourself crashing into
an empty seat or into the back of a person sitting in it. Once I had a large lady across my back
when I was using the seat in question. Only once!'

The Astoria closed on 5 January 1974 for subdivision. The Regal closed six weeks later and
Purley was without a cinema for two months. The Astoria's organ was saved by the East Kilbride
Organ Society and installed in the Ballerup Hall in the Scottish town's Civic Centre (it was
replaced by a Wurlitzer in 1977 and removed to the City School, Sheffield). Bryan Prosper
remembers: 'My last visit to the Astoria before its change to three screens was a full house on

Part of the upstairs auditorium of the Cannon (ex-Astoria) Purley after subdivision. (Photograph by Keith Skone.)

a Saturday night for *Doctor Zhivago*. When the lights went up at the interval, I looked up at the round disc lights under the circle, one of which I was directly under. There, on the inside of the light, were four mice running round and washing their faces. I was surrounded by young girls. I said nothing.'

Films returned on Sunday 14 April 1974 when the Astoria 1 opened *Swallows and Amazons* in the old circle area, seating 438, with a new screen and proscenium arch installed forward of the old one. The existing projection room was used but downstairs a new box served Astorias 2 and 3 which followed on Sunday 26 May in the former front stalls area. Astoria 2, seating 135, started off with *The Dove* and Astoria 3, seating 120, made its debut with *Enter the Dragon*. The entrance foyer now had a new lowered ceiling in plain modern style. A pub called The Painted Wagon occupied the former rear stalls area. Only the upstairs cinema retained any decorative features, with the capitals to the pilasters still lighting up on the side walls.

On 26 October 1978, a fourth cinema seating only seventy-six and using video equipment was opened in the old café area. In 1985, the Astoria passed with the rest of the EMI circuit to the Cannon Group. After Thursday 10 July 1986 the video cinema was closed, having proved unreliable and visually unsatisfactory. The name of the cinema was later changed to the Cannon and it became one of the only two cinemas in the Borough of Croydon. Cannon came under the same ownership as the American company Metro-Goldwyn-Mayer (MGM), leading to many Cannons, including Purley from 14 May 1993, being renamed MGM Cinemas.

Then the Cannon chain was acquired by Virgin, which disposed of most of the older cinemas including Purley. These formed a new ABC circuit which revived the old triangle logo as its trademark with the Purley cinema taking the ABC name from 7 June 1996.

As the ABC, the cinema closed on Thursday 13 May 1999, having been sold, before planning permission had been granted, for a replacement building that promised space on the ground floor for leisure use, including possibly a cinema. However, the old building was demolished in early 2000 and replaced by the striking Astoria Court which also takes in adjoining property on the corner of Whytecliffe Road South. No leisure use is evident. Solicitors Streeter Marshall occupy the area at No. 12 Purley Parade where the cinema entrance stood. The rest of the development is six floors of flats entered on the corner at No. 116 High Street. Here, set in the pavement, is an attractive mosaic depicting cinemagoers watching Clark Gable and Claudette Colbert in *It Happened One Night* on the silver screen with what looks like a representation of James Stewart in *Mr Smith Goes to Washington* to one side (see page 125).

four

Purley
Way

This wide view of the Warner Purley Way shows it rebranded Warner Village on the sign on the wall at left, although the impressive vertical Warner name sign on the glass tower proved resistant to change. It has since had a further change of name to Vue. (Photograph by Allen Eyles.)

Warner Cinemas/Warner Village Cinemas/Vue, Valley Park Leisure Complex, Lathams Way

The Valley Park leisure scheme, next to IKEA's redevelopment of the distinguished but defunct Croydon B Power Station (1949, architect: Robert Atkinson), was very attractive to multiplex operators as it provided plentiful ground-level open-air parking space and easy access by car from a wide area. In late 1988, American Multi-Cinema (then the leading operator of multiplexes in Britain) wanted twenty screens on the site. When work started in autumn 1994, Warner Bros. had signed up for a £7 million eight-screen development at first-floor level. The official opening was at lunchtime on Wednesday 17 January 1996 with a film-cutting ceremony that featured the Mayor and Mayoress of Croydon and actress Julie Walters, followed by previews of new films for the invited guests. Public performances started two days later. Keith Skone notes: 'In fact, there had been screenings to the local community (largely with free tickets) from the Saturday evening of 13 January. Previously released films were shown, including *Clueless, Loch Ness* and *Jurassic Park*'.

Films started as early as 12.25 p.m. on weekdays with the principal opening attractions being *Seven, Dangerous Minds, Ace Ventura: When Nature Calls, Babe, Showgirls, Fair Games, Something To Talk About* and *Goldeneye*. Four other films had limited showings: *The Indian in the Cupboard* and *Pocahontas* at weekend matinees, and *The American President* and *Pulp Fiction* with some evening

Night view of the Warner Cinemas, Purley Way, in 1996 with some of the car parking space visible in front. Note how the lower part of the tall spire (originally intended to be a flagpole) is lit up from below at night.

or late-night shows. Saturday morning shows for kids were established from the day after opening, showing recent U and PG films. There were late shows on Fridays and Saturdays.

The cinema was impressive externally with a glazed tower which lit up at night and carried the Warner name on the front. This had an art deco look to it and was far more striking than another Warner multiplex opened outside Watford on the same day. There were tall windows to either side of the tower and a canopy with backlit panels naming the current attractions further added to the traditional, 1930s look of the new multiplex.

Keith Skone observes:

> There were no framed posters – in keeping with Warner's policy on its latest generation of buildings. A narrow entrance with central pay desks soon proved inadequate for coping with large crowds. Beyond lay the escalators and lift, taking customers to the first floor's high-ceilinged foyer, concession stands and amusement arcade. Warner Bros. cartoon figures, along with laser lights, created a 'family friendly' Warner product-orientated area.

The foyer was intended to suggest a giant film set with its hanging arc lamps, gantries carrying video monitors showing film trailers, lights projecting a moving shield logo on the floor and huge models of Warner Bros. 'Looney Tunes' cartoon characters – a style devised by the circuit's interior designer Ira B. Steigler and fully initiated a little earlier at its Leicester site. This came in for some criticism as being too childish for adult audiences.

'Passageways from the foyer led to all eight auditoria,' recalls Keith Skone. The auditoria were primarily grey/black in décor and had stepped seating, large screens and Dolby digital surround sound. Keith continues: 'Screens 1 to 4 were a mirror image of 5 to 8. Screens 4 and 5 were the largest with 396 seats in stadium style. Screens 1 and 8 each seated 253, 2 and 7 seated 205, and 3 and 6 seated 178'. The total seating figure was 2,064 – less than the Savoy and Davis had each fitted in a single auditorium. 'No house tabs were fitted – the aim was that an image would be on screen at all times. Before films began, there were projected slides advertising local businesses. At second-floor level, up a narrow concrete staircase, was the large H-shaped projection room which fed all eight screens. This was lavishly equipped with Cinemeccanica projectors, all the latest sound systems, and the ability to interlock projectors to enable one film to be shown in up to eight screens.'

After massive audiences on the opening weekend, the cinema took some time to build good attendances. Three chain restaurants were nearby while immediately adjacent was a 3,200-seat Ritz bingo club, Europe's largest, which featured weekly cabaret – Ken Dodd drew about 2,000 people. This has since failed, no doubt hindered by lack of easy access to public transport – no buses served the site and both the club and the multiplex cinema had been running for a year or more before the Croydon Tramlink opened a station, which was still half a mile away.

The multiplex was renamed Warner Village Cinemas from 28 March 1997, reflecting Warner Bros' new international partnership with Australian chain Village Roadshow. Originally advertised as being at Croydon, the cinema is now identified as being at Purley Way to distinguish it from the Warner Village multiplex which opened in the town centre. Both sites were renamed Vue following the sale of the Warner Village circuit in March 2003, this one taking its new name from Friday 23 April 2004, two weeks after its rival.

five

South
Norwood

Central Hall Picture Palace/Central/Rex, No. 110 Portland Road (corner of Stanger Road)

The first permanent cinema in South Norwood opened in 1910 as the Central Hall (although plans named it as the Electric Light Picture Palace and it is not centrally positioned but on the fringe of the town). It was built as a cinema with some 500 seats, including a balcony partly supported by a pillar underneath. The projection box was rather awkwardly located in one rear corner and special lenses were required to correct the picture on the screen. It was part of James Watt's south London circuit which included the Central Halls at South Croydon and Tooting Bec (the latter almost identical to South Norwood).

From the late 1930s, the cinema was more simply known as the Central. By this time it suffered from the competition of the new Odcon and the modernised Astoria (ex-New Gaiety), both of them better located. All three cinemas had 6d as their lowest price in 1938 but the other two went up to 2s whereas the Central's top price was 1s. It was operated by Miss R. Lever who also took over the Astoria during the war years. In the 1950s the Central was renamed the Rex but it still retained the rather obscure Erneman sound system and ranked well behind its two rivals. Seating was now 529. It closed during 1956.

In later years the building became the Portland Room, offering banqueting halls for wedding receptions, Rotary Club lunches, buffet dances, etc., divided into upstairs and downstairs suites.

The Central Hall Picture Palace at South Norwood in 1920. The building is still very recognisable and the cupola on the corner survives in 2006 although most of the windows have been filled in and a single-storey extension added on the side.

Its cinematic past was recalled by its Foyer Suite and Stalls Bar downstairs and its Circle Suite and Circle Bar upstairs and by its display of film stills on the stairs, although nothing survived inside of the original cinema decor. Outside, it retained its corner dome and the words 'Picture Palace' could still be detected high up on the frontage where they had been painted over. In recent times, the building turned into a discount furniture showroom but in late 2005 it was vacant and up for sale.

New Electric/Electric/Mascot/La Rosa/Electric/Regent, No. 44b Portland Road

Opened on Tuesday 7 February 1911, the New Electric was a local enterprise led by Philip George. It had a very narrow entrance on Portland Road which led down a passageway to an auditorium that ran further back, set to one side. There were 300 seats on a sloping floor, with the rows being staggered to provide a less impeded view of the screen. It opened from 6.30 p.m. to 11 p.m. with matinees on Wednesdays and Saturdays.

However, by as early as August 1911, the cinema had closed down. It re-opened after improvements on Monday 30 October 1911, but its licence lapsed after 1914. It re-opened once more in 1917, as the Electric Theatre. It was re-licensed as the Mascot in July 1919 when its seating was given as 340 and it also operated for a spell under the name of La Rosa in the mid-1920s.

The narrow white frontage of the Electric Palace at South Norwood can be seen on the right, by the child standing on the pavement, interrupting the line of taller two-storey buildings.

It was once again the Electric in 1928 though it nicknamed itself The Cosy to try and turn its small size, compared to South Norwood's other cinemas, to its advantage. It had closed by the early 1930s, probably beaten by the cost of adapting for sound, but a final attempt was made to run it again from 1934 as the Regent, seating 276. It closed for the last time around February 1935, obviously unable to compete with its rivals.

Like the Norbury Cinema, it became a 'civic restaurant' during the Second World War, offering cheap meals, and it was later used for preparing school meals. From March 1963, it became a youth centre called the Socco-Cheta Club. By the 1990s, the former auditorium had a flat floor and false ceiling, and was divided up into three rooms for snooker, television and so on. The former projection room remained, reached by stairs outside and used for storage. In 2005, the Socco-Cheta Club closed and the building has been put up for sale.

New Gaiety/Astoria, No. 45 High Street

The New Gaiety was built near Goat House Bridge which crosses the railway. An enterprise of F. and G. Foster in association with H. Hammond, South Norwood's third cinema opened on Thursday 1 December 1921 with *The Dumb Girl of Portici* starring Madame Pavlova, *Mystic Faces,* an oriental tale featuring Jeff Abbe, plus Charlie Chaplin in *Shoulder Arms.* The auditorium was set at right angles behind a double gabled frontage divided between a shop and cinema entrance at street level. It had 750 seats including a small balcony. The most expensive seats (at 2s 4d) cost nearly five times as much as the cheapest seats at 6d. (By 1927 prices had been reduced, ranging from 5d to 2s.)

The New Gaiety had an organ which, writes Tony Moss, 'was built by the 'father' of the theatre organ, Robert Hope-Jones, although it predated his emigration to the USA, his revolutionary ideas and subsequent involvement with the Rudolph Wurlitzer Company, and was not a theatre organ as such. It had thirteen speaking stops on two manuals, and came from the Music Room of Sir August Manns (musical director at the Crystal Palace from 1855 to 1907). It was opened by Reginald New, beginning his distinguished theatre organ career at this cinema. The organ was eventually removed to the Church of St Mary of Nazareth, West Wickham'.

This newspaper advertisement contains the only known interior photographs of the New Gaiety (later Astoria) South Norwood. Note the bare screen, common at the time.

Above: The New Gaiety, *c.* July 1928. The double-gabled frontage is split between a shop and the entrance at street level. (John Gent Collection.)

Right: As later modernised to become the Astoria. This shot was taken shortly after closing when the new occupants have taken advantage of the display lettering. To left, out of view, a short glass tower, illuminated from within, was mounted on the frontage, extending vertically from first-floor level. (CTA/Tony Moss Collection.)

The New Gaiety was modernised and re-opened as the Astoria on 15 March 1937, the improvements being spurred by the impending arrival of South Norwood's Odeon. The frontage was clad in faience tiles and a small, vertical, pearl glass tower with metal frame drew attention to the building from the town centre. The architect was Richard Seifert, who went on to become one of London's most prominent architects (Centre Point et al).

During the Second World War the Astoria was damaged on three occasions and forced to close from late 1941 to 23 March 1942 and at other times. It came under the same management as the Central. To try and recover audiences eroded by its most recent closure, the management introduced Sunday night amateur talent contests in 1946. These were tried again to boost attendances from Sunday 22 May 1949. Auditions were held in the morning and Charlie Drake is said to have been one of the performers who tried out here.

Programmes were usually changed twice weekly (Sunday for four days, Thursday for three days) and were either second run or minor new films, as the Odeon was the only cinema in South Norwood with access to important new releases. The Astoria was soon losing money and even the closing of the Rex (the former Central) did not help.

The Astoria shut down on Saturday 13 July 1957 after a three-day run of *Mister Cory* starring Tony Curtis, supported by *Rock Pretty Baby* – a programme which had played for a week at the Odeon three months earlier. Owner Robert Lever said that he had lost £300 over the last six weeks and a lot more over the past five years, blaming rising costs, entertainments tax, and lack of access to first-run programmes. However, the cinema had not kept up with the times and is remembered as having gas primary lighting in the 1950s which was turned down by usherettes as the show started.

The building became home to Gipsy Hill Garages, using the foyer as a shop and the auditorium to store tyres and other spare parts. By the 1990s it had been thoroughly modernised and named David House. Only some decorative balustrading on stairs leading to the first floor remained from its cinema past. The old auditorium had been split horizontally, the Norwood Snooker Hall operating upstairs with a completely modern decor while the ground floor was offices, reached by an entrance around the side near where the front stalls would have been. In 2005, the upper part is offices while the lower area is the home of a religious group, the Higher Ground Assembly.

The Odeon South Norwood in 1937. The side of a small vertical name sign can be seen at top left, facing Norwood Junction railway station close by. There was a car park behind the cinema. (All Odeon South Norwood photographs by John Maltby.)

The main foyer of the Odeon South Norwood in 1937. Note the Odeon name set in the rubberoid flooring.

Odeon, Station Road

The Odeon was the sixteenth of thirty-six newly built additions to the Odeon circuit during 1937. The London and Home Counties branch of the Cinematograph Exhibitors' Association, the powerful trade body, had opposed it, arguing that it would put both the Astoria and Central out of business (which, of course, it didn't). It opened on Monday 26 July 1937, the same day as the Odeon at Crewe. The first film here was a special preview of *Talking Feet* with a personal appearance by dancing star, Hazel Ascot. The circuit's founder, Oscar Deutsch, also made an appearance during the opening ceremony which was attended by Andrew Mather, head of the architectural practice which designed it. Despite the volume of activity, the Odeon cinemas were designed to a high standard and the South Norwood Odeon was an excellent example of the now-celebrated circuit style. Built at a cost of £31,562, it was one of the best of Mather's many Odeons (better than his Odeon at nearby Penge which followed a few days later). It was the one really modern, large commercial building erected in the centre of South Norwood in the 1930s, and it greatly enhanced a very drab area.

The frontage was nicely proportioned with a gentle curve and plain cladding in vertical strips of cream-coloured vitrolite crossed by horizontal bands in jade green above the black

Above: the circle lounge of the Odeon South Norwood in 1937. Note the distinctive pattern of the carpet, along with the standard style of sofas and ash stand. The lower part of the decorative grillework on the frontage can be seen through the window. *Below:* the auditorium.

Above: This 1937 view of the auditorium of the Odeon South Norwood shows the colourful screen tabs of a Mediterranean village and one of the distinctive Odeon clocks on the side wall. As in the preceding shot, the concealed lighting in the frame to the ante-proscenium area has not been switched on and the appealing ambience of the auditorium is not fully brought out. This lighting still worked, in red, when the cinema closed. Below: British Thomson-Houston projectors in the box.

base. Interest focused in daytime on the decorative grillework in the central recess. At night, the Odeon blazed a welcome with neon on the horizontal green bands and on the red name signs, one of which was mounted on the side wall to face Norwood Junction station. There was a small car park for a hundred vehicles at the rear, reached from Cargreen Road.

The foyer was entered through double doors. It was shallow but wide with the paybox set in the far wall between the entrance doors to the stalls. Steps led up to the circle on each side (in later years, those on the right were blocked off and a sales kiosk installed across the bottom. The Odeon seated 1,572 – 1,020 in the stalls and 552 in the circle. All the seats were the same with padded arm rests, but those in the balcony had more space between rows and were, of course, stepped to provide a better view.

As with the frontage, simplicity was the key to the auditorium's design. Ribs around the proscenium arch directed the eye towards the screen. There were originally three sets of curtains, the inner screen tabs having a very colourful depiction of an Italian village (various imaginative designs were used by the circuit – this one also appeared at the Odeons at Bury and Lowestoft). The middle set of curtains was only used on special occasions and probably not motorised. The orchestra pit barrier was in an art deco pattern. The ventilation system made use of a neat grid of openings (each shaped like the octagonal 'O' of the Odeon trademark style of lettering and placed between the horizontal ribs to the side of the proscenium opening) and an opening covered by decorative grillework in the middle of the ceiling. There was a wood dado and one of the circuit's distinctive clocks on each side (these used the 'O' shape of the Odeon trademark with the letters of ODEON in place of numerals on the clockface) The whole ante-proscenium area was lit up by concealed lighting from the outer rim, changing from green to blue to amber during intervals.

The weekly Odeon release played here concurrently with the Odeon Croydon and ensured good attendances for many years. In the 1950s, a huge CinemaScope screen was installed in the proscenium arch and some of the front stalls seating removed. The rest of the stalls was re-spaced, reducing capacity to around 1,400. The inflexible programming was sometimes a weakness which resulted in some very poor releases – and when the Odeon did break ranks for a two-week special engagement of *The Ten Commandments* in September 1960 (two years after its run at the Odeon Croydon), it missed playing two popular releases, *Doctor in Love* and *Psycho*, but did not backtrack to pick them up. Declining attendances led to afternoon performances being discontinued except on Wednesday and Saturdays and during school holidays, while the circle never opened before 5 p.m.

The Odeon closed on Saturday 20 February 1971 after a week's run of double bill *They Call Me Mister Tibbs,* starring Sidney Poitier, and *Hornet's Nest,* starring Rock Hudson. As it was half-term, there had been separate matinees from Monday to Friday of a recent western more suitable for children, *The Hallelujah Trail.* (Saturday morning children's shows continued up to closure.)

The cinema had been little altered over the years (although the green neon outside was never replaced after the war and the stencil decoration on the auditorium walls had long been painted over) and it was looking run-down. The auditorium lighting and external neon name sign had not been changed. With some new carpet and a new coat of paint, it would been as inviting as when it opened. Apparently, the site was leased from Eagle-Star and the lease had expired or come up for renewal. It was acquired by a company called Mayfell Holdings and demolished along with adjacent property to make way for a dreary grey brick Safeway supermarket which has become a branch of Somerfield in 2005.

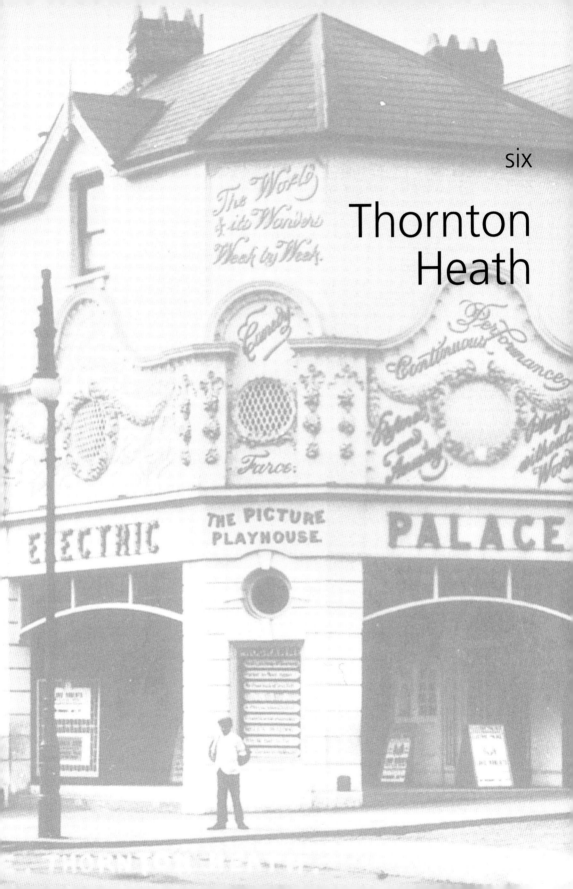

six

Thornton
Heath

Electric Palace, No. 48 High Street/The Retreat

Opening on Wednesday 23 March 1910, Thornton Heath's first cinema was a venture of one of the early British circuits, Electric Palaces Ltd, which then also operated Electric Palaces at Marble Arch, Brixton and Lewisham in the London area. It had further Electric Palaces under construction at Clapham and Hammersmith, and sites at Cricklewood, Highgate, Notting Hill, Putney and Stoke Newington.

An existing corner property was adapted to provide the entrance and the 700-seat auditorium was built up the side road called The Retreat, set back from the building line. There was also a tea lounge where the customary dainty teas were served. In order to encourage patrons from Croydon, they were offered a refund of their fares (except on Saturdays and holidays) at the end of 1910.

The arrival of the better-sited and more prepossessing Central made life difficult for the Electric Palace. Both cinemas came under the same ownership, leading to the closure of this one in October 1923 by the current owner, W.A. Martin, to concentrate business on the other.

In 1927 the Electric Palace was turned into a Palais de Dance with a sprung floor, thought to be the first in South London. In later years the corner entrance became home to a Coin-Op Seagull laundrette, but from the1990s it has been used by estate agents. The former auditorium became a furniture showroom for John Blundell Ltd. The original curved ceiling with its plasterwork and decorative bands was still intact above a low false ceiling. In 2005, the corner is occupied by estate agents Kingsbury while a short row of terraced houses has replaced the auditorium.

Above and opposite above: Thornton Heath's Electric Palace, offering, 'The World & its Wonders Week by Week'. The recess on the corner at ground level has the titles of the various shorts making up the programme. The lettering above the entrance describes the range of subject matter, including mirth, drama, tragedy, travel and sport. (CTA/Tony Moss Collection.)

Below: The Electric Palace Thornton Heath adapted to dance hall use. (CTA/Tony Moss Collection.)

This early view shows the Central at right and the clock tower in the distance at left – this alone still stands in 2005. The Pavilion name was later displayed horizontally in individual letters mounted across the arch above the entrance steps. (John Gent Collection.)

Central/Pavilion/Pullman, Nos 88-92 High Street, corner of Grange Park Road

Despite the existence of the Electric Palace, there were two proposals for further cinemas in Thornton Heath at the beginning of 1911. Plans were passed, against local opposition, for the Central and for a cinema in Brigstock Road. One of the protestors, a Mr Blackman, contended that cinemas were a curse because many people from the lower classes went night after night, leaving them with no money when the rent collector called.

Two new cinemas were at least one too many, and only the Central was built. It opened on Tuesday 17 October 1911, seating 580 on one floor. Boasting a small orchestra, it charged one shilling for reserved seats with others at 3d and 6d. The Central obtained the exclusive local right to show Kinemacolor pictures, as seen at London's Scala Theatre, and these formed the opening attraction.

By 1913, both the Central and the Electric Palace were controlled by Electric Palaces Ltd. By March 1914, Messrs. E. Palfrey & Co. operated the two halls, with Electric Palaces Ltd going into receivership soon after. Although, with standing room, the two cinemas could hold 1,600 between them, queues were reported outside the Electric Palace in 1914 (perhaps only for the cheaper seats). The Central closed for several weeks of structural alterations and improvements in 1921, re-opening on Boxing Day as the Pavilion. It then had an orchestra of six players to accompany the silent films for the evening performances. In 1923, the year that the Electric Palace closed, the Pavilion was largely avoiding British films because of their poor standing with patrons.

The Pavilion found a comfortable niche in the 1930s, sufficiently distant from the new State cinema on the London Road side of Thornton Heath to retain its own local audience. When German bombs demolished a row of shops next door in the autumn of 1940, the cinema was also damaged.

The former Central/Pavilion as the Pullman in 1956.

Programmes were changed on Sunday, Monday and Thursday with films being shown months after they had first been seen in central Croydon, but now of course at lower prices for the local audience that had missed them or was prepared to wait. In 1950, seating had been reduced to 481 (compared to 570 in 1932). The sharp fall in attendances in the 1950s particularly affected late-run cinemas like the Pavilion which had declined into something of a fleapit. The current operators, R.B. Cinemas, installed a wide screen early in 1955 (but not CinemaScope). Sunday shows were discontinued from July 1956 and the cinema closed altogether on 1 September 1956, a week after the Palladium in Croydon.

That, rather surprisingly, was not The End. It became a new addition to the small Pullman circuit which operated repertory cinemas at Brixton, Herne Hill, Bromley and elsewhere. Money was spent totally modernising the frontage (the open steps to the old paybox were enclosed by doors) and a new wide screen was installed in front of the narrow proscenium arch.

Re-opening as the Pullman took place on Tuesday 15 July 1958 with a revival double bill of *Witness for the Prosecution* and *Spring Reunion*. As at other Pullmans, programmes generally ran for an entire week, which was too long for Thornton Heath. The new lease of life lasted only nine months. During this period, the Pullman's weekly takings ranged from £14 to £96, and more than £3,500 was lost. It became cheaper to close down and pay the rent than to stay open. One of the last bookings – Norman Wisdom in *The Square Peg* – lost £39. Closure took place on Saturday 18 April 1959 after a week's run of *Kings Go Forth* supported by *Son of a Stranger*.

In 1960, there was an extraordinary proposal by one Peter Otter to re-open the place as a Palace of Varieties but by 1961 it had become a do-it-yourself shop. For a great many years, the entrance and two side shops formed the Handyman Shop (with timber and furniture stored in the auditorium). In 1985, the front section was converted into the Tasty Bite Pizza and Burger Inn (the steps inside were those formerly used by patrons to reach the paybox). The auditorium, now reached through exits on the side road, became a furniture warehouse for D.F. Webber and Harrison with a workroom built on supports in the middle of the floor. The projection portholes, the curved ceiling, the proscenium arch, and the red and gold decorative scheme of its Pullman days could still be seen. For many years after closure, fragments of posters (one clearly belonging to *Timberjack*, shown 9-11 June 1955) still lingered where they had been pasted on the side brickwork in Grange Park Road.

The auditorium was demolished but the front section continued as a fast food outlet for some further time. However, this too has gone and the area occupied by the cinema is now one end of the big new Leisure Centre for sport and exercise.

State/Granada, No. 793 London Road

The State was the fourth and last cinema to be designed, directly built and operated by the Australian-born A.C. Matthews, following the Rialto and Albany at Upper Norwood and the State at Sydenham.

It became quite common in the 1930s for new cinemas to appear on main roads some distance from a town centre, where large sites were more readily available and car parks could be provided. The State was located a mile from the centre of Thornton Heath on the busy London Road between Norbury and Croydon, very near Thornton Heath Pond (since filled in – the building was originally to have been called The Pond Cinema). Parking space was provided at the rear and to one side of the theatre.

The State had the most attractive frontage of the four Matthews cinemas with its tall windows framed in grey marble. The name sign was mounted on the front of the canopy. Inside the entrance doors were payboxes on both sides and fountains in the foyer. A café was located in the circle vestibule. The auditorium was large – with seating for 1,893 patrons – and had a rather old-fashioned curved ceiling with bands across it. There were wall panels decorated with pastoral scenes in 'semi-silhouette' painted by a local amateur artist.

The 20ft stage was deep enough to accommodate an orchestra and there were facilities to fly scenery and drapes as well as five dressing rooms. There was no orchestra pit or organ. The original screen tabs were in silver-grey with three wide vertical bands in petunia velvet to match the upholstery on the seats and the screen was originally positioned near the rear of the stage.

The Borough Engineer and the Licensing Committee consented to inspect the State on the morning of Boxing Day, Monday 26 December 1932, so that the cinematograph licence could be released and the cinema opened by the Mayor of Croydon at 2.30 p.m. The first attraction was *Speak Easily* with Buster Keaton, supported by *Divine Love* with Alexander Carr, plus Herman Danewski and His Band live on stage. Matinee admission prices were 7d for the stalls and 1s for the circle. Evening prices were 9d and 1s for the stalls, with three prices for the balcony: 1s 3d, 1s 6d and 2s.

Despite its size and modernity, it played pictures at least a week and more often a month after they had been shown in central Croydon. Programmes were usually changed midweek. It was leased by the small Blue Halls circuit in 1933. In 1934 and 1935, variety was being added on Friday nights only. At the end of the decade, it was being booked and operated by its original

Above and below: The Granada Thornton Heath. *Above:* taken on 16 February 1960. (Photo Coverage.)
Below: from mid-1950s as seen from The Pond, which was by this time filled in as a garden.
(D.R. Williams.)

proprietor, A.E. Matthews, before being sold to a company called AOC on 8 October 1940. Its fortunes changed dramatically when, in May 1948, it was bought by the powerful Granada circuit. Before the end of September, the State had dropped split-week second runs in favour of the weekly south London Gaumont programme, commencing with *If Winter Comes*, interspersed with occasional 'exclusives' or special bookings. The Davis Theatre in the centre of Croydon now had a powerful competitor often showing the same programme.

The State was renamed the Granada from 1 January 1949. 'Prior to the renaming,' Tony Moss recalled, 'there was much publicity in the neighbourhood in the form of bill-posters proclaiming "We are now GRANADA. Please pronounce it GRA-NAH-DAH." The new Granada signs were excellent, consisting of a red neon sign across the frontage and two yellow-lettered (but red neon) vertical signs at each end of the frontage. These could be seen from a long way away at night, particularly from the top of a bus going along Beulah Hill, Upper Norwood'. The side wall of the Granada rose above the older buildings on the north side of the Pond and another red neon sign was placed near the stage end of the building to catch the attention of traffic going round the Pond.

When CinemaScope with stereophonic sound arrived, the Granada was only a day behind the Davis in introducing it to the area, playing the same attraction, *The Robe*, from 9 August 1954. The installation cost £10,000, of which stereo sound accounted for £3,477: this issued from three banks of speakers behind the screen and eighteen other speakers spread around the auditorium. The largest possible screen was fitted within the 44ft-wide proscenium arch. There was no longer room for side-opening curtains. New 'reefer' curtains were fitted that rose and descended – as did the new side masking strips that reduced the width of the screen for ordinary wide screen. The Granada now had 1,885 seats.

The new screen was very effective for CinemaScope but it was far from ideal otherwise. The ordinary wide screen cut off far too much of the image top and bottom, particularly noticeable in the local advertising and in film credits unless the projectionist racked the image up and down to reveal all the information.

The Granada became part of the independent 'fourth circuit' that showed 20th Century-Fox's CinemaScope output, falling back on the Gaumont release in most other weeks. There was a bus stop right outside the cinema and this writer recalls the rush from the auditorium at the end of the evening performance before the National Anthem came on – not so much disrespect for the monarchy as the desire to get a good position in what often became an enormous bus queue.

After the fourth circuit faded away and a new 'Rank Release' was introduced in 1959 in place of the old Odeon and Gaumont releases, the Granada remained in a strong position with access to the Rank release of the week and generally played it concurrently with Rank's Odeons in Croydon, Streatham and South Norwood, and the Astoria Purley.

A 'Miss Candy' shop was built on one side of the foyer to supply sweets, soft drinks and cigarettes, with an exterior entrance that blocked a former emergency exit from the balcony, requiring a new exit and steps to be built on the side of the building. By the 1970s, the canopy had been taken down and the vertical neon sign replaced by one that spelt out the name in seven boxes illuminated from within.

As attendances declined, the Granada suffered from being somewhat out on a limb and the owning company's enthusiasm for bingo led to its closure as a cinema on 1 July 1972 after a week's revival of *The Italian Job* plus *Monte Carlo Or Bust*. The Granada re-opened as a bingo club on 13 October 1972 with a vertical sign reduced to five boxes that read BINGO. (On the side of the building at the stage end, the old-style cinema sign with red neon outline continued to spell out the Granada name.) Following the May 1991 management buy-out of the Granada bingo chain, signs renaming it Gala were erected on 4 March 1992. The club's viability seemed

The Granada Thornton Heath. Auditorium shot, with festoon curtain raised to show
CinemaScope screen, 11 January 1955 (Photo Coverage).

The Granada Thornton Heath: view across the auditorium, 26 May 1972.

The Granada
Thornton Heath, 26
May 1972, with its
later style of vertical
name sign.

seriously threatened by the new Ritz bingo hall in the Valley Park Leisure Centre off Purley Way but it was the Ritz that failed and the former Granada continues to play host to the eyes-down brigade in 2006. It has the only large surviving cinema auditorium in the Borough of Croydon. Although the stage has been opened up to bingo, table seating has been installed downstairs and the lighting scheme has been changed, it is still possible to stand at the back of the balcony where the cinema seats remain and sense its past when films were shown. This writer will never forget the thrill of seeing CinemaScope here for the first time, especially the short *Vesuvius Express* with the sound of the train roaring through the side wall speakers.

seven

Upper Norwood

The three main cinemas in this section were on the other side of the road from the Borough of Croydon but are included because they would have drawn much of their audience from within the borough. An early fourth cinema further away at Crystal Palace is included for the sake of completeness.

Photodrome/Electra/Electric/Palladium, Ranger Road (now Jasper Road) and (later entrance) No. 63 Westow Hill

This building started life as a swimming pool. It was converted around 1909 into a cinema called the Photodrome by putting a false floor over the basin. Projection came from behind the screen where (according to historian John M. East) a water pipe was used to spray the screen to keep it cool, the heat from the equipment evidently posing a problem. 'If the pressure was too high the water seeped through and splashed those people seated in the front row,' reported East in an article published around 1973, who added that the cinema, 'also had "Lover's knot seats" for courting couples, more interested in love making than watching the films'. The cinema was at this time entered on Ranger Road (since renamed Jasper Road), and had exits onto an open-air public passage on the other side.

The hall was soon taken over by three gentlemen, 'by no means strangers to the theatrical profession' (to quote a trade paper). They were Messrs Crossler, Taylor and Arthur Harold who redecorated and re-opened the cinema under the name Electra in early September 1909 with 500 seats and room for 200 standing. In 1912, a new, more conspicuous entrance was created through a former shop on the high street at No. 63 Westow Hill, providing a long, narrow interior passage down steps to reach the auditorium which was at a much lower level.

The Electra had become the Electric by the mid-1920s. It fell on hard times with the opening of the large, purpose-built Rialto and Albany cinemas a few minutes' walk away. It changed its name to the Palladium and closed in 1933. Re-opening took place on 26 November 1935 when back projection was still in use. In less than a year it had shut for good. In September 1937, the auditorium was re-opened by Mrs J. Arthur Rank as the studio of the Religious Film Society, funded by her Methodist husband to produce films for showing in churches. Guests were shown sets erected for filming and there was mention of a film library.

Left and opposite: The Electric Upper Norwood – photograph, *c.* 1923 taken from a programme cover, showing Harold Lloyd cut-out and posters for Norma Talmadge in *The Eternal Flame*. And in the mid-1920s with giant bottles supplied by the distributor to help promote the film *Wine*. The downward steps of a public passageway are just evident to the left.

Much later, the premises became a warehouse for the Jacatex mail order company. In 1973, John M. East reported that tiles from its swimming pool days lined the walls and that the proscenium arch of the old cinema was still there. By 1986, the former auditorium had become the Crystal Palace Snooker and Social Club with an entrance on Jasper Road as in earlier days. It has since been completely replaced by new housing. The entrance on Westow Hill for many years housed a tobacconist's and a laundrette. Together with adjacent shops, it has recently become a Budgens outlet. The passageway to the left has long been closed off.

Crystal Palace Cinema/Picture House, Crystal Palace

A Cinematograph Theatre became one of the side shows in the west wing of the famous Crystal Palace from June 1910 with no separate admission fee. The Crystal Palace Cinema opened in 1920 with the post-war return of the Palace; it charged for admission and was located in an area that, before the war, had been used as a variety theatre.

It was then renovated and re-opened as the Crystal Palace Picture House on Monday 28 September 1925 with the documentary *The Epic of Everest*. Films were shown six days a week with two changes of programmes. Admission prices ran from 6d to 1s 10d. There was plentiful parking space for cars. It closed on 8 March 1930 for sound equipment to be installed but never re-opened – the management of the Crystal Palace had financial difficulties and the two modern cinemas in Upper Norwood must have drawn audiences away. Subsequently the Crystal Palace was largely destroyed in one of the most spectacular fires of the 1930s.

In the late 1990s, the site was to house a 20-screen, 4,600-seat UCI TheFilmWorks 'megaplex', but determined local opposition on environmental grounds happily put paid to what would have an oversized and visually unappealing development.

Rialto/Granada, No. 25 Church Road

Such was the rush to open cinemas that they very often made their debut with parts unfinished, and a film trade writer considered it worthy of note that the Rialto stood fully completed on the first night, Saturday 6 October 1928. This may have been because the architect, builder and proprietor were one and the same: an Australian called A.C. Matthews. The cost of the 1,393-seat cinema was put at £10,000. The entrance space immediately behind the outer doors occupied an unusual semi-circular area as the inner set of doors was placed in a curve. A particularly distinctive feature of the auditorium design (as far as British cinemas were concerned) was the saucer shape of the stalls floor with the front rows on a rise – this was considered to give a better view of the screen. The film on the opening day was *Ramona* starring Dolores Del Rio. Film stars Anna May Wong and John Stuart were there in person to help with the opening ceremony – Miss Wong addressed the audience with a few words in Chinese.

The Rialto was a little on the chilly side to judge from later advertising that additional heating had been installed. There was a first floor restaurant. Western Electric sound was introduced in 1930 and the Rialto coasted along as the foremost cinema in Upper Norwood. Mr Matthews consolidated his hold on the local film-going market by building a further cinema, the Albany, in Upper Norwood, and the State a mile away in Sydenham. He also built the State at Thornton Heath.

Left: The Rialto is seen in 1948, still prominently advertising its luncheons. and (*opposite*) in March 1955 as restyled by Granada.

His two Norwood cinemas and the one at Sydenham were taken over by Excelsior Super Cinemas in the early 1930s and later became part of the Medway Cinemas circuit of eight halls which was acquired by the Granada chain in March 1949. The architectural practice of George Coles was brought in to modernise the Rialto which was renamed Granada from Monday 11 September 1950. The restaurant was retained. The Albany became the Century.

The week's south London ABC circuit release was usually booked into the Granada but the Odeon or Gaumont release would be programmed if that was particularly strong. The Granada was far enough away from the Odeon South Norwood and Regal (Gaumont) West Norwood to play the same films, especially when it was part of such a go-getting circuit.

From February 1961 the cinema advertised itself as the Granada Crystal Palace rather than the Granada Upper Norwood. It outlasted the Century and seemed in a strong programming situation. But it closed on Saturday 26 May 1968 after a week's run of *Reflections in a Golden Eye* supported by *Assignment to Kill*. Like many other Granadas, the cinema was turned over to bingo, re-opening on 27 June 1968 – but this was short lived, the club closing in July 1969. The building was then re-opened by an independent bingo operator as the Lesleen Social Club on 9 February 1970. When this closed, Granada had another try at bingo – with such success that it went on to become part of the group taken over by Gala in May 1991 and given the new owner's name. It remains a Gala bingo hall in 2006, remarkably little altered from its cinema days.

The entrance hall of the Granada Upper Norwood (*above*), March 1955, showing curved inner set of entrance doors and the addition of the circuit's style of chandelier. *Below:* view in opposite direction taken in November 1951 with stairs to balcony and doors to stalls at right. (Photo Coverage.)

Above and below: The auditorium of the Rialto Upper Norwood around 1948 when taken over by Granada.

The auditorium of the Granada Upper Norwood in March 1955 when the circuit's distinctive chandeliers had replaced the earlier light fittings in the ceiling.

This exterior view shows the Century 'temporarily' closed in the summer of 1958 with the taller Granada beyond. The roofs of the two buildings meet at right angles. The brick side wall of the Granada on Church Road was partly concealed by large advertising hoardings. (CTA/Tony Moss Collection.)

Albany/Century, No. 18 Church Road

A.C. Matthews, the proprietor of the Rialto, wisely feared that another cinema operator would build a cinema in Upper Norwood to the detriment of the Rialto and so he quickly designed and built the Albany, opening it on Saturday 18 January 1930 with *The Glad Rag Doll,* starring Dolores Costello, and *High Society,* starring Laura La Plante. The next day the cinema was closed (a license for Sunday opening had been refused) and on Monday *Smiling Irish Eyes* ran for six days.

The Albany was put up on derelict land in a mere fifteen weeks (claimed as a world record). A smaller, less luxurious building than the Rialto, it seated 1,250 on a single sloping floor with a tiny foyer. Amber tapestry panels were the main decorative features of the auditorium, said to be in a modem French style. There was no stage but an orchestra pit was provided. The entrances of the Rialto and Albany were a short distance apart, but the back wall of the Rialto (behind the screen) met the side wall of the Albany where the auditorium extended straight back.

Both the Albany and Rialto were taken over by Excelsior Super Cinemas within two or three years. The Albany was remodelled to plans of C. Edmund Wilford in 1937, reducing its seating to 970. Tony Moss recalled: 'The Albany was unusual for a 1930s cinema in that it had only one pair of tabs. They were very attractive, having a gazebo as the central feature with a border of flowers right across. I remember two light standards on each side of the stage, if you could call it that, which lit up in the interval'.

This interior photographs shows the Albany in 1950 during reconstruction for re-opening as the Century.

Another view of the Albany in 1950 being prepared for re-opening as the Century. (CTA/Tony Moss Collection.)

On the outbreak of the Second World War, the Albany closed and was requisitioned as a government food store. The building was released in July 1948 and re-opened as a cinema in October of that year. Along with the Rialto, it was soon acquired by the Granada circuit which closed it for reconstruction. Re-opening took place on Boxing Day 1950 and it was now called the Century, the name given to secondary cinemas run by Granada.

The best programme of the week played the larger Granada, so that the Century was in an inferior position unless there were two good shows available. In September 1957, the Century dropped weekday matinees other than on Wednesday – always an ominous sign. From the following month, the manager of the Granada, Ken Jarvis, also ran the Century as a further economy. Once it became evident that there was insufficient support for two cinemas, this was the obvious choice for closure. After a week's run of a feeble ABC circuit release, *The Young Invaders* (supported by a revival of Chaplin's *The Kid)*, the Century closed on Saturday 30 May 1958 for 'a rest period'. A recent bus strike had hurt attendances and a shortage of first-run films was claimed. Although there had been references to an autumn re-opening, this never happened.

From late 1960 until 1988 it became car showrooms for Selhurst Park Garages and carried the name Century House, recalling its cinema days. A good impression of the original auditorium could be still obtained from the surviving plaster decoration on the side wall and the ceiling grille. It continued displaying cars for sale as Century House under S.G. Smith but all traces of its cinema past were wiped out by a thorough refurbishment in late 1988. In late 2005, the building stands closed and boarded up.

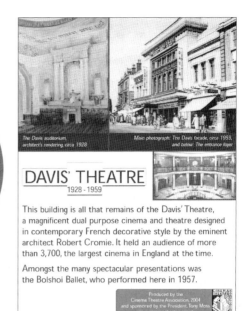

IN THE
DAVIS THEATRE
WHICH STOOD ON THIS SITE
SIR THOMAS BEECHAM Bt.CH.
CONDUCTED THE
FIRST PERFORMANCE OF THE
ROYAL PHILHARMONIC
ORCHESTRA
ON
SUNDAY 15th SEPTEMBER
1946

The Davis auditorium, architect's rendering, circa 1928

Main photograph: The Davis facade, circa 1959, and below: The entrance foyer

DAVIS' THEATRE
1928 - 1959

This building is all that remains of the Davis' Theatre, a magnificent dual purpose cinema and theatre designed in contemporary French decorative style by the eminent architect Robert Cromie. It held an audience of more than 3,700, the largest cinema in England at the time.

Amongst the many spectacular presentations was the Bolshoi Ballet, who performed here in 1957.

Produced by the Cinema Theatre Association, 2004 and sponsored by the President, Tony Moss www.cinema-theatre.org.uk

IN MEMORIAM

The Davis Theatre is incidentally recalled by the plaque (*above left*), mounted on the office block at the back of its former site. (Photograph by Allen Eyles.) The Davis is properly remembered by this plaque (*above right*) erected next to the former entrance to the Davis Theatre Croydon by the Cinema Theatre Association. *Below:* this cinema-going mosaic is in the pavement outside the flats on the site of the former Astoria Purley. (Courtesy of Richard Norman.)

Index

Other local titles published by Tempus

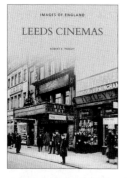

Brighton and Hove Cinemas
ALLEN EYLES

This fascinating collection of over 150 photographs provides a unique view of the cinemas of Brighton and Hove. In 1896 Brighton became the first town outside London to show films and it has had a remarkable range of picture houses over the years. These include the Regent, the most spectacular cinema in the country when it opened in 1921, and the Astoria, with its French Art Deco interior.

0 7524 3069 6

Leeds Cinema
ROBERT E. PREEDY

With over 200 old photographs, programmes and advertisements, this book provides a fascinating look at the history of cinema-going in the city of Leeds and its suburbs over the last hundred years. It includes chapters on the technology behind the silver screen and the entrepreneurs and cinema chains which operated in the area. The images in this book will delight all those who have fond memories of visiting some of Leeds' picture houses, many of which disappeared long ago.

0 7524 3583 3

Cinemas and Theatres of Wandsworth and Battersea
PATRICK LOOBEY

Cinemas and Theatres of Wandsworth and Battersea is an illustrated history that brings to life the places that occupied a warm place in the hearts of London's theatre-going public. This fascinating and informative gazetteer-style volume of the known venues in the area is illustrated with over 100 black and white images and contains a colour section of some of the area's best and brightest venues and advertisements.

0 7524 3356 3

Bristol Cinemas
DAVE STEPHENSON AND JILL WILLMOTT

Through the medium of old photographs, programmes and advertisements, this book provides a fascinating look at the history of cinema-going in the city of Bristol and its suburbs during the last century. From mobile cinemas to penny gaffs, this A-Z of cinemas in Bristol chronicles the places frequented by Bristolians over the years, including the ABC on Whiteladies Road, the Magic Box in Stokes Croft and the Picture House in Knowle.

0 7524 3669 4

If you are interested in purchasing other books published by Tempus, or in case you have difficulty finding any Tempus books in your local bookshop, you can also place orders directly through our website

www.tempus-publishing.com